Poetry Lessons

to Meet the Common Core State Standards

Georgia Heard

SCHOLASTIC

New York • Toronto • London • Auckland • Sydney
Mexico City • New Delhi • Hong Kong • Buenos Aires

Dedication

To my sisters—Lisa, Jacqueline, and Patty

Acknowledgments

This past spring, I had the pleasure of speaking at a wonderful conference in Athens, Greece. Despite the current economic hardships and turmoil, Athens is one of the most beautiful cities I've visited, and its people some of the friendliest. One afternoon as I was wandering around the streets, I was struck by how one minute I saw a Starbucks on a modern-looking street built up with shops and the usual urban traffic, and then I turned a corner and suddenly saw the most magnificent ancient columns of a ruin—the library of Hadrian built in the second century AD—rise above me, the modern and the ancient existing side by side.

Similarly, teaching feels like that—we continuously build layers of experience and knowledge that we acquire over the years. My teaching poetry work began many years ago in a different city, New York, as a graduate student at Columbia University and extended to my staff development work in the city's schools with the Teachers College Reading and Writing Project. Over the past 20 years, I've had the privilege of visiting many amazing schools in the United States, as well as around the world, and I'm grateful for everything I've learned from the students, teachers, and administrators in all the places I've worked.

I specifically want to thank the following schools where the student examples cited in this book come from: The Benjamin School in North Palm Beach, Florida; The Wilson School in St. Louis, Missouri; and The Hong Kong International School.

Just like the layers of ancient history in Athens, I will keep the voices and faces of all the students, teachers, and administrators I've had the pleasure to work with over the years in my heart and mind. Thank you for your inspiration, and for the opportunity to do teaching work that's so filled with joy.

Credits: Every reasonable effort has been made to trace the ownership of all copyrighted poems. Any errors which may have occurred are inadvertent, and the editors and publisher will gladly make the necessary correction in subsequent editions. "Enchantment" by Joanna Ryder © 1990 by Joanne Ryder. "Ears Hear" by Lucia M. Hymes and James L. Hymes Jr. from OODLES FOR NOODLES © 1964 by Lucia and James Hymes Jr. "Sound of Water" by Mary O'Neill from WHAT IS THAT SOUND! ©1966 by Mary O'Neill. "We Are Trees" by Francisco X. Alarcón © 1997 in LAUGHING TOMATOES: AND OTHER SPRING POEMS by Franciso X. Alarcón. Published by Children's Book Press, 2005. "When I Was Lost" by Dorothy Aldis from ALL TOGETHER © 1925–1928, 1934, 1939, 1952, © renewed 1953–1956, 1962 by Dorothy Aldis, © 1967 by Roy E. Porter. "Saturday" from DID YOU SEE WHAT I SAW? by Kay Winters. Copyright © 1996 by Kay Winters. Used by permission of Viking Penguin, a division of Penguin Group (USA) Inc. "Ice Cream Cone" by Heidi E. Y. Stemple. Reprinted by permission of Curtis Brown, Ltd. "Sand House" by J. Patrick Lewis. Reprinted by permission of the author. "A Modern Dragon" by Rowena B. Bennett from SONGS FROM AROUND A TOADSTOOL TABLE © 1967 by Rowena Baston Bennett. "Ditchdiggers" by Lydia Pender from MORNING MAGPIE © 1984 by Lydia Pender. "A Circle of Sun" and "Dragonfly" from LEMONADE SUN AND OTHER SUMMER POEMS by Rebecca Kai Dotlich. Copyright © 1998 by Rebecca Kai Dotlich. Published by Wordsong, an imprint of Boyds Mills Press. "Ode to the Washing Machine" from IN THE SPIN OF THINGS: POEMS OF MOTION by Rebecca Kai Dotlich. Copyright © 2003 by Rebecca Kai Dotlich. Published by Wordsong, an imprint of Boyds Mills Press. "Ducks on a Winter's Night," "Eagle Flight," "Song of the Dolphin," "Favorite Bear," and "Bat Patrol" From CREATURES OF EARTH, SEA AND SKY by Georgia Heard. Copyright © 1997 by Georgia Heard. Published by Wordsong, an imprint of Boyds Mills Press. Reprinted by permission. "My Horse and I" by Georgia Heard. From SONGS OF MYSELF: AN ANTHOLOGY OF POEMS AND ART by Georgia Heard. Published by Mondo. Copyright © 2000 by Georgia Heard. Used by permission of the author and Curtis Brown, Ltd. "Oak Tree" by Georgia Heard. From FALLING DOWN THE PAGE: A BOOK OF LIST POEMS by Georgia Heard. Copyright © 2009 by Georgia Heard. Published by Roaring Brook Press. Reprinted by permission of the author. "My People" from THE PANTHER AND THE LASH by Langston Hughes. Reprinted from THE COLLECTED POEMS OF LANGSTON HUGHES. Copyright © 1994 by the Estate of Langston Hughes. Reprinted by permission of Alfred A. Knopf, an imprint of Random House, Inc.

Cover design: Maria Lilja
Interior Design: Sarah Morrow
Development Editor: Joanna Davis-Swing
Editor: Sarah Glasscock
Copyeditor: David Klein

ISBN: 978-0-545-37490-3
Copyright © 2013 by Georgia Heard.
All rights reserved. Printed in the U.S.A.

5 6 7 8 9 10 11 12   40   19 18 17 16 15 14

CONTENTS

Poetry and the Common Core State Standards

Several years ago I read an article in *Newsweek* announcing that poetry is dead. Because of our fast-paced lives and increasing reliance on instant communication—cell phones, texting, e-mail—poetry, the article said, is old-fashioned and slow. It takes effort and time to deliver its message.

As an antidote to *Newsweek*'s pessimistic announcement, I read recently that poetry, as an art form, may predate literacy. Poetry was the means by which prehistoric and ancient societies told and retained stories of their culture. In some ways poetry still serves this purpose, and it is also the genre that best represents our inner lives. I believe that even during these fast-paced times, poetry will survive—probably longer than *Newsweek* will.

I don't remember reading poetry as a child, but I remember hearing poems. My mother would recite nursery rhymes and verse: "Pease porridge hot/Pease porridge cold/Pease porridge in the pot/Nine days old," and "Mairzy doats and dozy doats and liddle lamzy divey. A kiddley divey too, wouldn't you?" My mother didn't sit down and explain the meaning of "Pease porridge hot" or "Mares eat oats." It didn't matter. I loved my mother, and it was the sound of her voice, and the music of the words, that made me fall in love with poetry.

In *The Well-Tempered Critic* (1963), Northrop Frye wrote:

The infant who gets bounced on somebody's knee to the rhythm of "ride a cock horse" does not need a footnote telling him that Banbury Cross is twenty miles northeast of Oxford. He does not need the information that "cross" and "horse" make (at least in the pronunciation he is most likely to hear) not a rhyme but an assonance. He does not need the value judgment that the repetition of "horse" in the first two lines indicates a rather tin ear on the part of the composer. All he needs is to get bounced. If he is, he is beginning to develop a response to poetry in the place where it ought to start.

Now, with the Common Core State Standards (CCSS) adopted by nearly every state, and its emphasis on poetry's more pragmatic cousin—informative and explanatory writing—I fear that poetry might not survive in schools. I'm grateful to the authors of the CCSS that reading poetry is included, however. Even if poetry is shared initially to meet academic standards, I hope that children will gain the benefit of poetry's pleasure and power.

The CCSS states that one of its goals is to prepare students for college and careers in the 21st century. I believe it's fair to ask what poetry's role is in this preparation. Will students need poetry in their careers? Will they need poetry in college if they aren't planning to become scholars, teachers, or professors of literature? (I suppose we can ask the same question about all literature.)

As I pondered that question, I heard a keynote by one of my educational mentors. He said that he had visited a classroom recently and the teacher was teaching *onomatopoeia*. He said to her, "Why are you teaching them onomatopoeia? Are they going to be academics? How are they going to use this?"

Many of the teachers in the audience clapped.

I thought to myself that poetry is still misunderstood. *Onomatopoeia* comes from the Greek word meaning "word making," and it has been used in stories and poems for centuries. When I've taught onomatopoeia, children love the idea that a word like *bang* or *clap* is called something as interesting and strange as "onomatopoeia."

When young children listen to nursery rhymes like "Baa Baa Black Sheep" or "Pease Porridge Hot," they are listening to onomatopoeia. When the little train in *The Little Engine That Could* goes, "Chug, chug, chug. Puff, puff, puff . . . the little train rumbled over the tracks," that's onomatopoeia. When high school students read "Brrrriiiinnng! An alarm clock clanged in the dark and silent night" in Richard Wright's *Native Son*, they are reading onomatopoeia.

Perhaps onomatopoeia is not the most essential literary element, but it's an example of a literary device that gives us ear pleasure and adds to our authentic experience of a story, song, or poem.

One of the most eloquently stated reasons for including poetry in schools comes from the Massachusetts English Language Arts Curriculum General Standard:

> *From poetry we learn the language of heart and soul, with particular attention paid to rhythm and sound, compression and precision, the power of images, and the appropriate uses of figures of speech. And yet it is also the genre that is most playful in its attention to language, where rhyme, pun, and hidden meanings are constant surprises. The identification and analysis of the elements generally associated with poetry—metaphor, simile, personification, and alliteration—have an enormous effect on student reading and writing not only in poetry, but also in other genres.*

From poetry we learn the language of heart and soul. No one is going to write a résumé with the language of poetry, but there are many enjoyable life experiences that reach beyond our career paths and help us become more well-rounded, compassionate, and empathetic human beings.

Poetry is part of our common cultural language. It would be a sad day if we forgot Maya Angelou's powerful and defiant "Still, I Rise": "You might write me down in history/With your bitter twisted lies"; or Langston Hughes's poignant and poetic question, "What happens to a dream deferred?"; or the rhythmic cadence of Robert Frost's "Whose woods these are I think I know."

We want students to develop a habit of being readers of all genres—a habit based on enjoyment, wonder, and amazement—that extends beyond college and career. The CCSS attempts to set out a vision of what it means to be a literate person in the 21st century, and part of that vision is for students to partake in close, attentive, critical reading that is at the heart of understanding and enjoying works of literature including poetry, as well as reading texts to create an informed and critical citizenry. Lucy Calkins and her colleagues write about critical reading skills: "It is essential work, actually, for anyone who wants to be a knowledgeable citizen. Every time we vote, we sift through candidates' stories. Often as we read the news, we ask ourselves, Who wasn't included in this story?" (Calkins, Ehrenworth, & Lehman, 2012).

But close reading of a poem doesn't mean overanalyzing a text by spending a month reading one poem, which doesn't guarantee a deeper understanding. The Billy Collins poem "Introduction to Poetry" speaks about analyzing a poem by tying ". . . the poem to a chair with rope/and torture a confession out of it." We have to be careful not to read poetry for the sole reason of satisfying and checking off a CCSS standard. Instead, we need to teach our students to read poetry for the sheer joy of it, and then invite them into a deeper study of poetry.

In *The Reader, the Text, the Poem: The Transactional Theory of the Literary Work* (1978), Louise Rosenblatt proposes that there are two kinds of reader and text transactions: efferent and aesthetic. An efferent reading stance, which asks students to read for facts and information and to analyze and synthesize that information, is becoming more predominant in schools as testing and standards become central to education and a motivating force behind teaching. The second stance, aesthetic, involves reading with a focus on feelings, thoughts, and images; the reader shapes meaning from a text from personal experiences, emotions, and images. But interpreting a poem requires readers to go back to the text for support of their explanations, and to pay attention to the details.

In writing this book on poetry and the CCSS, I'm aware that, because poetry appears in the standards, we have to be careful not to shift our reading of poetry to a completely efferent stance. If we read poetry only to satisfy the expectations in the CCSS, then we're doing poetry a great disservice, and missing the heart of poetry.

Denise Levertov (1968) warns against taking the life out of poetry: "The would-be poet who looks on language merely as something to be used, as the bad farmer . . . looks on the soil . . . merely . . . to be used, will not discover a deep poetry."

If we approach poetry this way, students' responses to it will be what many of our own responses to poetry have been in the past—they will groan at the mention of it. Reading poetry will become shallow and routine, and students will walk away with a dislike and fear of poetry that so many people have.

We need to read poetry for the sheer pleasure of it. We need to read poetry to learn the language of heart and soul. We need to read poetry with Rosenblatt's aesthetic stance. But it doesn't mean that we can't learn about the craft of poetry, and that we can't balance between an aesthetic and efferent stance once we've fallen in love with a poem. Poetry is a powerful teacher and motivator for all of our students. Poetry teaches us about the power of language to transform our experiences, but it can also teach us about wordplay, point of view, tone, and rhythm.

Novelist and short story writer Grace Paley once wrote, "I really went to school on poetry. I learned whatever I know about language and craft from writing poems" (Bach & Hall, 1997). Well, I believe that the same can be said for reading poetry. Instead, Grace Paley might have written, "I went to the school of reading poetry in order to learn how to read prose."

WHAT POETRY TEACHES STUDENTS

Here are some additional reasons to include poetry in your classroom.

- Poetry demonstrates rich, precise, imaginative language.

- Poetry's short, spare, and concise format is often more manageable to read, especially for struggling or reluctant readers, and enhances confidence and reading motivation.

- Poetry can provide a brief, and sometimes much-needed, break from daily routines.

- Through poetry students can practice inferential thinking in text that is short yet filled with meaning.

- Poetry gives voice to children's feelings about themselves and the world, and helps them make a personal connection to literature.

- Poetry can help create a more relaxed and positive classroom atmosphere.

- Poetry is a highly effective way to promote fluency.

- Poetry's range of subject matter is vast and varied, and can help build children's interests and create new ones.

Overview of Poetry in the ELA Common Core State Standards

The CCSS is not meant to be a grade-by-grade poetry teaching guide; the standards are more like signposts to guide teachers toward a deeper study of, in this case, poetry. *Poetry Lessons to Meet the Common Core State Standards* is meant to be a road map on this journey that will honor the heart and the breadth and depth of poetry, and guide teachers in understanding the poetry component of the CCSS. Teaching the genre of poetry requires a greater understanding of the features of poetry than most of us gained in high school or college.

The CCSS expects students not just to know the genre of poetry but also the genres of prose and drama, and with that knowledge to be able to compare and contrast poetry's structural and craft devices with those of other genres.

The English Language Arts Standards are organized into seven categories with a K–12 grade-level progression. Since the standards spiral, progressing grade-by-grade and building on previous grades, it's important to know the standards in the grades below and above so you can build on that knowledge when introducing a new standard.

For the purposes of this book, I will focus only on the standards for grades K–5 that name poetry specifically, and craft elements that are commonly attributed to poetry (asterisked below). The charts on the following pages correlate the CCSS to the chapters in this book.

The writing standard is the only standard that does not mention poetry, although the CCSS states the following:

"The narrative category does not include all of the possible forms of creative writing, such as many types of poetry. The Standards leave the inclusion and evaluation of other such forms to teacher discretion."

But this doesn't mean that we shouldn't teach students how to write poetry. In my book Awakening the Heart: Exploring Poetry in Elementary and Middle School, *I explore in depth how to teach writing poetry and how reading and writing mirror each another. I do include information about writing poetry in this book, but only as a way to support students' reading comprehension.*

Categories of English Language Arts Standards

- Reading: Literature*
- Reading: Foundational Skills*
- Reading: Informational Text
- Speaking and Listening*
- Language*
- Writing
- Appendix A (Text Complexity) and Appendix B* (Text Exemplars)

1. Reading Standards for Literature K–5

Through the extensive reading of stories, dramas, poems, and myths from diverse cultures and different

time periods, students gain literary and cultural knowledge as well as familiarity with various text structures and elements. There are three main goals for poetry:

- For students to be exposed to a variety and range of poetry from different time periods, cultures, and voices in order to gain cultural knowledge
- For students to acquire and integrate knowledge of the craft and structure of poetry in order to better understand a poem's meaning
- For students to acquire critical reading skills in order to integrate and evaluate poems by comparing and contrasting craft, structure, and content across several genres

The College and Career Readiness Anchor Standards for Reading for Literature K–5 contain ten standards, which are divided into four main categories:

- *Key ideas and details* requires readers to read for details as well as for central ideas and themes.
- *Craft and structure* requires readers to read for craft and for how a particular poem conveys meaning through its craft and structure.
- *Integration of knowledge and ideas* involves students in making connections and comparisons across genres and across texts on similar topics.
- *Range of reading and level of text complexity* involves students in reading a variety and range of poems and levels of increasingly complex text as they progress through the grades.

Category	College and Career Readiness Anchor Standards for Reading: Literature (K–5)	Chapter/ Page Number
Key Ideas and Details	1. Read closely to determine what the text says explicitly and to make logical inferences from it; cite specific textual evidence when writing or speaking to support conclusions drawn from the text. 2. Determine central ideas or themes of a text and analyze their development; summarize the key supporting details and ideas. 3. Analyze how and why individuals, events, and ideas develop and interact over the course of the text.	Chapter 2, pp. 19–36
Craft and Structure	4. Interpret words and phrases as they are used in a text, including determining technical, connotative, and figurative meanings, and analyze how specific word choices shape meaning and tone. 5. Analyze the structure of texts, including how specific sentences, and larger portions of the text (e.g., a section, chapter, scene, or stanza), relate to each other and the whole. 6. Assess how point of view or purpose shapes the content and style of a text.	Chapters 4–7, pp. 44–81 Chapters 8–11, pp. 82–106

Category	College and Career Readiness Anchor Standards for Reading: Literature (K–5)	Chapter/ Page Number
Integration of Knowledge and Ideas	7. Integrate and evaluate content presented in diverse media and formats, including visually and quantitatively, as well as in words. 8. Delineate and evaluate the argument and specific claims in a text, Including the validity of the reasoning as well as the relevance and sufficiency of the evidence. 9. Analyze how two or more texts address similar themes or topics in order to build knowledge or to compare the approaches the authors take.	Chapters 3–11, pp. 37–106
Range of Reading and Level of Text Complexity	10. Read and comprehend complex literary and informational texts independently and proficiently.	Chapters 12, 13, pp. 107–113

Most of the poetry standards in the Reading Standards for Literature K–5 appear in the Craft and Structure category; however, beginning in grades 4 and 5, students are asked to determine the theme of a poem in the Key Ideas and Details category, which I address in Chapter 2:

- **RL. 4.2** *Determine a theme of a story, drama, or poem from details in the text; summarize the text.*

- **RL. 5.2** *Determine the theme of a story, drama, or poem from details in the text, including how characters in a story or drama respond to challenges or how the speaker in a poem reflects upon a topic; summarize the text.*

Chapters 4–11 offer demonstration lessons that specifically address Craft and Structure Anchor Standards 4 and 5.

2. Reading Standards: Foundational Skills

The Foundational Skills for Reading category focuses on four areas of "fostering students' understanding . . . of concepts of print," the alphabet, and other conventions. The purpose of these standards is to support and help develop proficient readers. Poetry is specifically named in this standard under Fluency in Grades 3–5 as a way for students to comprehend poetry and for teachers to support students as readers. Chapter 3 discusses fluency.

Category	Reading Standards: Foundational Skills (Grades 3–5)	Chapter/ Page Number
Fluency	4. Read with sufficient accuracy and fluency to support comprehension. b. Read on-level prose and poetry orally with accuracy, appropriate rate, and expression on successive readings.	Chapter 3, pp. 37–43

3. Speaking and Listening Standards

The third category in which poetry appears is in the Speaking and Listening Standards for grades 2 and 3. The purpose of two of these standards is to create opportunities for students to take part in a variety of rich, structured conversations—as part of a whole class, in small groups, and with a partner—as well as to include new technologies, such an embedded video and audio in expanding the role that speaking and listening play.

Category	Speaking and Listening Standards (Grades 2 and 3)	Chapter/ Page Number
Presentation of Knowledge and Ideas	**2.5** Create audio recordings of stories and poems; add drawings or other visual displays to stories or recounts of experiences when appropriate to clarify ideas, thoughts, and feelings.	Chapter 3, pp. 40–43
	3.5 Create engaging audio recordings of stories or poems that demonstrate fluid reading at an understandable pace; add visual displays when appropriate to emphasize or enhance certain facts or details.	Chapter 3, pp. 40–43

4. Language Standards

Poetry also appears in the Language Standards. One of the purposes of these standards is for students to be able to determine or clarify the meaning of grade-appropriate words they encounter through listening, reading, and media use, and to come to appreciate that words have nonliteral meanings, shades of meaning, and relationships to other words.

Although the Language Standards do not mention poetry per se, students are expected to understand nonliteral meanings of words and poetic devices such as figurative language, specifically metaphor and simile, which are common poetic devices also used in fiction, nonfiction, and drama.

Category	College and Career Readiness Anchor Standards for Language K–5	Chapter/ Page Number
Vocabulary Acquisition and Use	**5.** Demonstrate understanding of figurative language, word relationships, and nuances in word meanings.	Chapter 7, pp. 75–81

5. Appendix B: Text Exemplars

In each grade band (K–1, 2–3, and 4–5), the CCSS provides examples of poetry in two categories: poems to be read aloud (K–3) and poems for students to read independently (grades 4–5). The exemplar poems consist of a wide range of not only time periods but also cultures—from English poet Christina Rossetti, who wrote in the late 1800s, to contemporary Native American poet Alonzo Lopez, to popular contemporary children's poets such as Eve Merriam. These exemplar poems are referenced at the end of each demonstration lesson.

How This Book Is Organized

The first chapter, "Creating a Place in the Classroom for Poetry," describes how to create an environment for reading and writing poetry in the classroom. This chapter focuses on how and when to teach poetry and includes a menu of rituals and ways it can be integrated throughout the year.

Chapter 2, "Reading Poetry and the K–5 CCSS," explores reading comprehension through the use of various strategies; for example, living with a poem for one week, reading a poem on Poetry Fridays, and reading a poem through different lenses.

Chapters 3–11 follow pertinent standards in a grade-by-grade progression. Most chapters begin with an introduction to the standard; a demonstration lesson on how to teach it in the classroom, accompanied by a sample poem to use with the lesson; followed by specific classroom practices for Collaborative Engagement and Independent Application. The goal of the Collaborative Engagement and Independent Application section is to guide students in internalizing and integrating concepts taught in the demonstration lessons through partner and group work as well as through independent work. The activities in this section are also a means of assessing students' understanding.

In chapters 12 and 13, respectively, I address text complexity and the range of poetry in the CCSS.

The Appendix contains the following:

- a chart correlating the poems in this text to the CCSS
- reproducibles of charts and thinking maps
- a glossary of poetry-related terms

My goal in *Poetry Lessons to Meet the Common Core State Standards*, as always, is to help teachers and students grow in their understanding and love of poetry that will last a lifetime.

CHAPTER 1

Creating a Place in the Classroom for Poetry

My son begged me to buy him a pair of pet turtles one year. I agreed, and when we brought the turtles home, we realized that we had no idea what they needed to survive besides food and water. After researching on the Internet, we drove to the pet store to buy a heat lamp to supply warmth on cold days and nights, a plastic pond for the turtles to swim in, a ceramic bridge for them to cross or hide beneath, and several other items. A few dollars later, the turtles' habitat was ready to sustain two thriving and happy pets.

Extending this metaphor to the classroom, you can't read a poem occasionally and expect students to develop a deep appreciation, understanding, and love of poetry. First, we need to build an environment where poetry is part of classroom rituals and structures throughout the year, so students' experience with poetry is successful and their understanding grows over time.

How to Teach Poetry Across the School Year

Although the CCSS doesn't specify how to teach poetry—the focus of the standards is on results and expectations—how and when we teach poetry is just as essential as what we teach. This chapter will lay the framework of ways to include poetry during the year—and how to teach it to meet the CCSS.

What Do Students Already Know About Poetry?

Start your poetry exploration by talking with students about what they already know about the subject. Prompt the discussion by asking some of the questions below, and sharing your own thoughts and experiences.

- *What is a poem?*
- *Have you ever heard a poem before?*

- *Do you remember the poem or what it was about?*
- *Do you have a favorite poem?*
- *Can you say it?*
- *What do you like about that poem?*

On a large sheet of chart paper, begin to write students' responses. By having a conversation about poetry, you can gauge students' prior experience with it, which will inform your teaching. If, for example, most students can't remember ever listening to a poem, you'll want to begin by reading a variety of poems every day for several weeks to tune their ears to poetry. If most students have only heard or read poems by Shel Silverstein, and they believe that all poetry is humorous and silly, plan to read free-verse, nonhumorous poems that show a different side of poetry for a while.

Make Poems Visible

Like the Poetry in Motion project several years ago, in which poetry was displayed in public places (e.g., on subways and buses) in many cities around the United States, make poems visible in your classroom and around the school. If we make poetry visible—instead of poetry books sitting quietly on the library shelf, tucked away, waiting to be read—students will read poems every day, and those poems will become more familiar, accessible, and relevant to their lives. Try the activities below in your classroom.

Poetry Around the Room

To show students that poems are written about everyday things, find poems about common classroom objects (such as a stapler, a pencil sharpener, books, and so on), copy them on small index cards, and tape them to the corresponding objects in your classroom. Take a tour of the displayed poems, stopping to read each one, and then invite students to write their own poems about everyday objects. Display their work around the classroom, too. *School Supplies*, edited by Lee Bennett Hopkins, is an excellent anthology that contains poems about classroom objects.

Poetry Posters and Poems in Frames

Write several poems on large sheets of chart paper. Ask students to illustrate the margins, and then display the poems on the wall so they can be read throughout the day. Collect copies of favorite poems in anthologies.

You might also frame one of your favorite poems, or a class favorite, and display it on the wall. Doing this makes a powerful statement that we value poems so much that they deserve to be placed in a frame like a painting.

Poetry Books in Your Classroom Library

In order to have an ample supply of poetry books for read-alouds and independent reading, I recommend that you devote at least 20 percent of your classroom library to poetry. Gather poetry books in baskets and in bins, and categorize them by theme related to your content-area studies, or by a favorite poet, anthologies, poetry picture books, or novels in verse, such as Sharon Creech's popular *Love That Dog* and *Hate That Cat*. You can also copy a single poem on a sheet of paper and laminate it to include in poetry baskets.

Poems During Read-Aloud

When I gather students close to read a poem aloud, I usually write the poem on a chart, show it on a SMART Board, or give students copies so they can follow along as I read.

(However, there are times when I want students to close their eyes and visualize the poem without seeing the words as I read aloud. Listening to a poem strengthens students' listening skills—it supports visualization—and can help focus their listening on a poem's rhythm or rhyme.)

Read Lots of Poetry

Read. Read. Read. Students need to hear and read poems—lots of them: poems that rhyme; poems that make us clap our hands and dance to their rhythm; poems that paint vivid pictures of, for example, waves breaking on a shore or the whisper of fall leaves; funny poems that make us roll over with belly laughs; poems that speak to other feelings, such as sadness at losing a beloved pet, or shyness, or feeling lonely. Read Shel Silverstein and Jack Prelutsky, yes, but also read poems by other, perhaps less well-known, poets such as Arnold Adoff and Rebecca Kai Dotlich. Read poems by contemporary poets and poems written in other times and eras. Read poems from poets who live in other countries and cultures. Just as with music, we need to hear and read the full range of poetry.

The CCSS makes it clear that through reading both great classic poems and contemporary poems representative of a variety of periods, cultures, and worldviews, students can vicariously inhabit worlds and have experiences that differ greatly from their own. A wonderful anthology of contemporary poems from around the world to share with students is *This Same Sky* edited by Naomi Shihab Nye.

Since children's listening comprehension is stronger than their reading comprehension until the middle grades, reading poetry aloud is one of the ways we can introduce them to more complex text and help build knowledge toward the goal of independent reading.

Read poems aloud to the whole class, and encourage small-group and partner reading. During independent reading time, make sure there are plenty of poetry books and single poems available for students to read. The CCSS includes exemplar poems in Appendix B for read-alouds as well as for independent reading.

Encourage students in the older grades to read texts independently and reflect on them in writing in poetry response journals.

Consider weaving some of the following activities into your classroom routine to create an environment where poetry can grow and thrive throughout the year.

Read a Poem Aloud Every Day

Carve out a specific and predictable time every day to read a poem aloud: first thing in the morning, after students have unpacked and are getting settled, after lunch when they return excited and sweaty from recess, at the very end of the day before making the transition to home. It only takes a minute or two to read a poem.

On the next page is a sample schedule showing when you might read aloud a poem. I've also included suggestions for poetry books to read during a typical school day.

Classroom Poetry Read-Aloud Schedule

Time	Poems	Poetry Books
Morning meeting	Poems to begin the day, poems about morning, poems about school-related topics	*Wake Up, Sleepy Head!: Early Morning Poems (Poems For the Young)* by Mandy Ross; *If You're Not Here, Please Raise Your Hand: Poems About School* by Kalli Dakos
Weather check	Poems about weather and seasons	*Weather: Poems for All Seasons*, edited by Lee Bennett Hopkins; *Winter Eyes; Handsprings; Autumnblings; and Summersaults* by Douglas Florian
Language Arts class	Poems about reading, writing, speaking, books	*Wonderful Words: Poems About Reading, Writing, Speaking, and Listening* and *I Am the Book*, edited by Lee Bennett Hopkins; *BookSpeak! Poems About Books* by Laura Purdie Salas
Math class	Poems about math	*Marvelous Math: A Book of Poems* edited by Lee Bennett Hopkins; *Aritheme-Tickle: An Even Number of Odd Riddle-Rhymes* by J. Patrick Lewis; *Math Poetry: Linking Language and Math in a Fresh Way* by Betsy Franco
Lunch	Poems about food, lunch, eating	*Carrots to Cupcakes: Reading, Writing, and Reciting Poems About Food* by Susan M. Freese
Science class	Poems about science	*Spectacular Science: A Book of Poems* edited by Lee Bennett Hopkins; *Outside Your Window: A First Book of Nature* by Nicola Davies; *The Tree That Time Built: A Celebration of Nature, Science, and Imagination*, edited by Mary Ann Hoberman and Linda Winston
PE class	Sports poems	*Good Sports: Rhymes About Running, Jumping, Throwing, and More* by Jack Prelutsky; *And the Crowd Goes Wild! A Global Gathering of Sports Poems* edited by Carol-Ann Hoyte and Heidi Bee Roemer
End of day	Poems about homework, evening, going to bed, and sleeping	*Switching on the Moon: A Very First Book of Bedtime Poems* by Jane Yolen; *Sweet Dreams of the Wild: Poems for Bedtime* by Rebecca Kai Dotlich

Begin a What We Know About Poetry chart. As you read the daily poem aloud, have students point out which qualities of poetry they notice and add those to the chart.

Celebrate Poetry Fridays

Every Friday teachers around the United States celebrate poetry through Kidlitosphere, a connected link of children's literature blogs created and maintained by teachers. These bloggers review the newest children's poetry books, share favorite poems, and introduce inspiring teaching and writing ideas. If every classroom devoted just one hour on Poetry Fridays to poetry, students would be experts by April, which is National Poetry Month.

Use these suggestions to incorporate poetry into your classroom on Poetry Fridays.

- Read aloud poems to the class and during shared reading.
- Students read poems independently and in small groups.

- Students create anthologies of favorite poems.
- Students illustrate, perform, choral read, and tape readings of favorite poems.

Teach a Monthlong Unit in Reading and Writing Poetry

Spending a month reading and writing poetry will give students the ability to read a poem critically with depth and insight, and their writing of poetry will help build a foundation for writing in all genres. National Poetry Month in April is the perfect month to devote to poetry.

Build Poetry Anthologies Over Time

As you read poetry aloud, students can listen for poems that they love or that relate to their lives in some way and collect them in individual anthologies or a class anthology. Encourage them to illustrate any thoughts, memories, or mind pictures in the margins of the poem. Students can create anthologies of favorite poems as an ongoing project on Poetry Fridays or over a few weeks during National Poetry Month.

Begin by asking students if they know what an anthology is. Explain to them that *anthology* comes from the Greek words *anthos* (flower) + *logia* (collecting). Define a poetry anthology as a collection of poems by different poets (just like a bouquet of flowers). The anthologist and poet Paul Janeczko likens collecting poems to collecting baseball cards.

Flip through several anthologies, show students the titles, and discuss the theme of each collection. Display the table of contents, its organization, illustrations, and other pertinent features of the anthology.

Below are some tips for organizing individual or whole-class anthologies:

- Organize it around a single theme, such as sports, animals, or friendship.
- Organize it around a specific form (e.g., haiku or list poems), such as my anthology *Falling Down the Page: A Book of List Poems*.
- Organize it around a favorite poet, such as Langston Hughes or Shel Silverstein.
- Organize it around feelings: poems that make us laugh, poems that comfort, or poems that make us reflect and think.

Take Daily Poetry Breaks

Poetry is a great way to take a break during the school day. Stop the class and read a poem that will calm and relax your students. Ask students to close their eyes and see the imagery. Read poems and help orchestrate brief performances, snapping fingers and clapping hands to the rhythm of the poem. Read poems to deepen and personalize content-area subjects. Read poems that will make your students laugh and lighten their day.

Celebrate National Poetry Month

April is late in the year to introduce poetry. But if your schedule is extremely busy, and you can't find time to read poetry during the year, devote a lot of time in April to reading and writing poems.

CHAPTER 2

Reading Poetry and the K–5 CCSS

When my 99-year-old grandmother died, a friend created an anthology of poems about life and death for me. Although I had read several of the poems in high school and college, rereading the poems with the grief of missing my grandmother in my heart changed my reaction to them.

One of the poems was Robert Frost's "After Apple Picking," which I had studied in college and knew well:

> "My long two-pointed ladder's sticking through a tree
> Toward heaven still,
> And there's a barrel that I didn't fill . . ."

Intellectually, I knew the poem was about how the speaker contemplates his life's achievements by using the metaphor of a hard day's work of apple picking. But when I read it after my grandmother's death, I experienced the poem in a new way. I was older and understood life's regrets, challenges, and celebrations as Robert Frost must have when writing the poem, and as my grandmother certainly did at 99.

We can ask students to answer questions about a poem and ask them to find its theme or main idea, but until we feel, as Emily Dickinson wrote in a note, "If I read a book [and] it makes my whole body so cold no fire can ever warm me I know that is poetry. If I feel physically that the top of my head were taken off I know that is poetry." Dickinson reads and recognizes poetry by her physical response to a poem—she feels the poem as a way of finding meaning in it.

Edward Hirsch expresses a similar idea: "We activate the poem inside us by engaging it as deeply as possible, by bringing our lives to it, our associational memories, our past histories, our vocabularies, by letting its verbal music infiltrate our bodies, its ideas seep into our minds, by discovering its pattern emerging, by entering the echo chamber which is the history of poetry, and most of all, by listening and paying attention."

But this journey, this activating the poem inside us, is not encouraged by the CCSS. Eighty to 90 percent of the CCSS Reading Standards for Literature require a text-dependent analysis, which means that students are asked questions about a text that can only be answered by referring explicitly back to it—and not by exploring feelings, memories, associations, and background knowledge. One of the authors of the CCSS found in a research study of K–12 reading that 80 percent of the reading questions did not require students to go back to the text to answer them, which is what critical reading is about.

We need to strike a balance between an efferent and an aesthetic stance, especially when we first introduce poetry to students. When readers interpret a poem, they are encouraged to go back to the text for support of their interpretations. Students who are familiar with and fluent in reading poetry will be more motivated to analyze a poem line-by-line and go back to the text to explicate and answer questions about it.

Slowing Down the Reading of Poetry

After spending time exploring the breadth of poetry, we can begin to slow down our process of reading. Rereading a poem and uncovering layers of meaning, including our connections as well as our critical reading of craft and structure, is one of the great pleasures of reading poetry.

Most poems don't have stories or plots that will entice students to eagerly turn the pages to get to the next event in the story as fiction does, or interesting facts with bright and colorful photographs and graphics as nonfiction has. We read poems differently. Poetry asks us to ponder meaning, savor words, create images, and connect to our feelings. Slowing down our reading has nothing to do with literal speed but instead is about an artful reading—a close reading of a poem. Once students become familiar with a range of poems and feel comfortable with the genre, then we can begin to introduce ways to invite readers to examine and analyze a poem in engaging ways.

Billy Collins calls them, unpoetically, "retarding devices." He says, "That kind of spooling back in the poem to reread lines, reread the whole thing, that sense of inhabiting the poem's body you get when you're reading it on the page . . . I think that creates an intimacy with a poem that is lost in performance poetry" (Collopy, 2011).

In an interview about his book *The Art of Slow Reading* (2011), Thomas Newkirk writes, "So I think it's finding the kind of pace where you feel like you're totally engaged with the reading."

The Partnership for Assessment of Readiness for College and Careers' *PARCC Model Content Frameworks Road to Implementation* of the CCSS states, "A significant body of research links the close reading of complex text—whether the student is a struggling reader or advanced—to significant gains in reading proficiency and finds close reading to be a key component of college and career readiness." The English Language Standards Reading: Literature states that, "Students also acquire the habits of reading independently and closely, which are essential to their future success."

A line-by-line reading or close reading of a poem, and the verbal or written explanation and discourse about a poem, is called explication. **Explication** comes from the Latin word *explicare*: to unfold. It means to fold out, or make clear the meaning of, and usually involves a line-by-line and sometimes word-by-word reading and commentary on the structure, craft, and meaning of a poem, finding evidence to support our ideas, and referring to that evidence as we speak and write about it. Interpreting and explicating a poem is a dance between close reading and standing back to see the big picture, the theme of a poem, and then asking ourselves, So what? How and why does this poem matter to me? A close reading of a poem is, as Billy Collins says, an intimate reading of a text, a collaboration between writer and reader. It demands that we bring ourselves to the poem and that we read with both our hearts and our minds. Ultimately, we want a poem to open us to a new world, to remind us of our own deeper realm.

Rereading a Poem

It takes time to enter a poem's world. When we reread a poem, we peel back its layers and intensify our understanding and relationship to it. Most readers of poetry make the mistake of assuming that we should understand a poem on the first reading, and if they don't, there is something wrong with them or with the poem.

Students' comfort and confidence with poetry will help motivate rereading, but loving a particular poem is the best motivator of all. After all, what motivation would students have to reread and explicate a poem that they don't like, or feel that they'll never be able to understand?

Close reading of a poem involves teacher modeling and demonstrating specific strategies; for example, how to infer the theme of a poem or read the poem for craft. We should model what we do when we read a poem we love and make not just our thinking visible but also our full response: how we feel when we read the poem; what memories the poem evokes, as well as words and parts of the poem that puzzle us; observations of its craft and structure; words and lines we love.

Show students how writing directly on a poem can help us record and keep track of our thinking. We can model the following:

- sketching imagery in the margins of a poem
- having a conversation with a poem by writing associations and feelings that it brings to mind
- writing a question mark and/or circling words and lines we don't understand
- underlining rhyming and repeating words
- highlighting figurative language
- marking the meter and rhyme scheme

My Process of Rereading

Teachers can make their process of reading, not just of one but several different kinds of poems, visible. Then ask students to try independently to make their reading of a poem visible with a partner or small group.

When I make my own first-draft reading and rereading process of a poem visible, it looks something like this.

On my first reading I do the following:

- notice the way the poem looks on the page: the form of the poem, if it has stanzas, line length, how long the poem is, and how much white space surrounds the words

- notice who the poet is and if I know any other poems he or she has written
- read the title to see if it gives me any images or associations or helps me predict what the poem will be about
- read the whole poem and get the general gist of it
- see if I am willing to enter the poem's world
- visualize the poem's imagery
- ask myself if I feel an immediate emotional connection to the poem
- notice and take pleasure in the poem's craft
- notice any musical or sound patterns such as repetition, rhythm, or rhyme

On my second, and subsequent readings, I notice more details and deepen my reading of the poem by doing the following:

- slow my reading down line-by-line and word-by-word
- re-envision the poem's imagery to clarify meaning
- deepen my emotional connection to the poem
- savor the music and sounds of the poem
- reread lines and words I don't understand to clarify meaning
- understand the poem on a figurative level
- notice and reflect on the "constructedness" of the text—how it's built—as well as the poet's use of literary craft and why he or she constructed the poem that way
- reflect on the poem's meaning and message

Milan Kundera, quoting and extending Proust, writes, "Every reader, as he reads, is actually the reader of himself. The writer's work is only a kind of optical instrument he provides the reader so he can discern what he might never have seen without the book. The reader's recognition in himself of what the book says is the proof of the book's truth."

A Lesson on Rereading With First Graders

In a first-grade classroom, I began a mini-lesson by telling students that one of the things readers of poetry do is reread. We reread because poems are short, they go by quickly, and on the first reading, we get a basic idea of the poem, but in our second and third reading, we absorb more details and begin to understand the poem more completely.

I likened the reading of a poem to meeting a person for the first time. You might decide on that first meeting that you like the person, you notice the clothes he or she is wearing, you notice whether she or he is friendly, you notice how he or she talks. But on that first meeting, that person is not your best friend, yet.

The first time we read a poem we can get a general idea of it. We might decide if we like it or not, we might understand the poem, we might be reminded of something in our own lives, we might notice interesting or unusual words. But it's not until we read the poem a second, third, or fourth time that it becomes our friend—that we really begin to connect to it.

Then I gave each student a copy of "Ducks on a Winter's Night" from my collection *Creatures of Earth, Sea and Sky: Animal Poems*. At the bottom of the poem, I had drawn two boxes and numbered them. I asked students to follow along as I read the poem aloud, and to pay particular attention to the mind pictures the words made them see. I did not do any prereading discussion on vocabulary or background knowledge.

After the first reading, I asked the first graders to draw their mind pictures in box #1 at the bottom of the poem. Then I asked students to follow along again as I reread the poem and to pay attention to any details they might not have noticed on the first reading and to draw a second picture, including those new details in box #2. One student's work is shown at the right.

The difference between the first and second drawing, the first time reading the poem and the second, is distinct. In the first reading, the student drew several of the poem's details in pencil: the zzzz's show that the duck is sleeping; the moon and a star show that it's night. But this student's understanding of the poem, as shown in his drawing, is tentative and sparse.

> ## :: Ducks on a Winter's Night ::
> ### by Georgia Heard
>
> Ducks asleep
> on the banks of the pond
> tuck their bills
> into feathery quills,
> making their own beds
> to keep warm in.

After the second reading of the poem, the drawing in box #2 comes to life through color and detail: he drew several ducks instead of one (Ducks asleep); he drew the blue wind blowing to show that it's cold because it's winter time ("Ducks on a Winter's Night"); and the quarter moon shines a yellow column of light down next to the ducks.

The stark contrast between this reader's first and second reading of the poem is visual evidence of how essential rereading a poem is to understanding details more accurately and developing a more complete understanding of the whole poem.

Living With a Poem for One Week

Rereading one poem for a week invites readers to slowly climb deeper inside its meaning. Subsequent readings will support students in asking and answering questions about key details, and over the week, they will come to a deeper understanding of a poem, such as determining the theme. In *Climb Inside a Poem: Reading and Writing Poetry Across the School Day* (2007), my co-author, Lester Laminack, and I write about how to slow down and savor a poem for one week. It only takes 5–15 minutes a day (depending on the poem and the grade) to read and discuss the poem. You can live with a poem for one week periodically throughout the school year—for example, every other week, or once a month—to build students' knowledge of poetry.

Read the poem aloud, or have students read it with a partner or in small groups, and as the week progresses, they will gradually unfold details and features that they didn't notice the first time they read. Students can also read independently, or for homework, and record their changing responses to the poem in their poetry response journals and then share these responses in class.

Below is a sample template for living with a poem for one week, along with a variety of ways to guide students in close reading of a poem. Each day for a week, or less, depending on the grade and the type and complexity of the poem, read aloud or have students read the same poem independently or in small groups. After reading, model how readers gradually draw evidence from a text and glean meaning from it.

When you introduce Living With a Poem for a Week, be sure to tell your students that getting at the heart of some poems might take weeks, months, or in some instances, even a lifetime. Exploring a poem and finding its meaning can be a slow process. It includes not just determining what the poem is about but also what we, as readers, bring to that understanding: our own images and experiences, and knowledge of the genre.

Monday: Introducing the Poem

On the first day, read the poem aloud and have students follow along. In discussing the poem, begin with an open-ended response, focus on what the poem says, associations and feelings students have about the poem, and any special features it has.

A menu follows, listing possible questions to model in a think-aloud as you discuss a poem with students. You can model your own thoughts before, during, and after you read by writing on a chart next to the poem or on a sticky note. (Be sure not to overwhelm students by asking or exploring all of the questions; instead, select the questions that are most appropriate to the type of poem and the students you're teaching.)

Before Reading

- *Let's take a quick glance at the poem. What do you notice?*
  Long or short lines?
  Does it have any stanzas? (See Chapter 11 for a demonstration lesson on stanzas.)
  What kind of stanzas?
  Is the poem long or short?

- *Read the title: What clues does the title give us about the poem?*
  When you hear (or read) the title, what pictures do you see in your mind?
  Can you predict what the poem is about from the title?
  What do you already know about this topic?

- *Read the poet's name: Do you know the poet?*
  If you do, what kind of poem do you expect? A funny poem? A rhyming poem? A nature poem?

During and After Reading

Read the poem all the way through first for students to get the gist. Then reread line-by-line

and pause at preselected stopping points (after each stanza or after a complete image or thought) to ask and answer questions.

I'm going to stop here and ask:

- *What picture is the poet painting in your mind?*
- *What do you understand from what we just read?*
- *What does the poem make you feel?*
- *Are there any words that stand out to you?*
- *Do you have any questions about the poem?*
- *What do you think the structure of the poem is?*
- *What type of poem is it? Free verse? Traditional with rhyme and stanzas?*

The next day's reading and discussion will depend on what students noticed and discussed the previous day.

Tuesday and Wednesday: Reading Deeper: What Does the Poem Say?

Now that students have read the poem once and discussed what they noticed, model what readers do when rereading a poem:

- *In my mind, I see a picture of a _____ . These are the words/lines that give me a picture in my head.*
- *I'm wondering about this word and why the author chose to use this particular word.*
- *I want to think about what the main idea of the poem is. I think it is _____ because _____. Any thoughts about this?*
- *I noticed that the poet repeats these words _____. I'm wondering why the poet did this.*

RL. 2.1 states: "Ask and answer such questions as *who, what, where, when, why,* and *how* to demonstrate understanding of key details in a text." To fulfill this standard, you can also focus Tuesday and Wednesday on the *who, what, where, when, why,* and *how* of the poem. Exploring these types of questions gives students ways to climb deeper into the details and eventually the meaning of a poem.

Answering *who, what, where, when, why,* and *how* questions is a doorway toward understanding the heart of a poem. We can ask students, for example, how does knowing the *what* and *where* of a poem help us understand its message? How does exploring the *why* help us understand its theme? If answering questions becomes rote and seems like just another assignment, it will not enlighten students' understanding of the poem.

It's helpful to think of these questions in two categories: closed questions and open questions. Closed questions (*who, what, where*) usually require short responses that are found directly in the text (*Where does the poem take place? What happens in the poem?*) Open questions (*why, how, what if*) demand more in-depth answers that are not explicitly stated in the text and require

> *The CCSS states that:*
>
> *Surprisingly, what chiefly distinguished the performance of those students who had earned the benchmark score or better from those who had not was not their relative ability in making inferences while reading or answering questions related to particular cognitive processes, such as determining main ideas or determining the meaning of words and phrases in context. Instead, the clearest differentiator was students' ability to answer questions associated with complex texts.*

the reader to voice an opinion (*Why did the poet write this poem? How is the poem made? What if . . . ?*).

As students reflect on these questions, they can write down evidence and details to support their thinking in their poetry response journals. Or they can record the information on a 5W and H Thinking Map (see the sample on p. 27) to use as evidence in a discussion about a poem. (A reproducible is on p. 116.)

Closed Questions

Who?

The who in a poem can be interpreted in two ways: as the person(s) named in the poem or the person who is speaking the poem. They could be one and the same.

Here are some questions to think about when exploring the speaker of a poem. (Remember, the speaker of the poem is not necessarily the poet.)

- *Who is speaking? Can you tell the gender, age, or anything else about the speaker?*

- *Does the speaker have a distinctive voice?*

- *What attitude does the speaker have toward the subject of the poem?*

- *Are any words written in dialect?*

- *What is the speaker's voice like—familiar, conversational, formal?*

- *Is the poem a **dramatic monologue**?*

- *What point of view is the poem written in—first, second, or third person?*

- *Why does knowing who the speaker is matter? How does knowing about the speaker help us understand the poem's message?*

What?

- *What's happening in the poem? Is there action? A story? Or does the poem express a feeling, an observation, or a thought?*

- *Can you retell or summarize the poem?*

- *Why does knowing the "what" matter? How does knowing the what of the poem help us understand its message?*

Where?

- *Where does the poem, or the events in the poem, take place? In an actual place, such as a baseball stadium or the beach, or in a more universal place?*

- *Identify which details tell us where the poem takes place. Which words or lines tell you where it takes place?*

The Reading Literature Standards for grade 5 requires students to understand how the speaker of the poem reflects upon a topic:

RL.5.2 Determine the theme of a story, drama, or poem from details in the text, including how characters in a story or drama respond to challenges or how the speaker in a poem reflects upon a topic; summarize the text.

The Language Standard for that grade states:

L.5.3 Compare and contrast the varieties of English (e.g., dialects, registers) used in stories, dramas, or poems.

- *Why does knowing the "where" of the poem matter? How does knowing the where of the poem help us understand its message?*

When?

- *When is the poem taking place? In an unspecified or universal time, or in a specific time or era? A particular season or time of year?*
- *How do you know when the poem takes place?*
- *Why does knowing the "when" of the poem matter? How does knowing the when of the poem help us understand its message?*

Open Questions

Why?

- *Why did the poet write the poem? What's the purpose of the poem? To tell a story; to express a feeling; to give an observation of the world; to persuade, give courage, make us laugh, share a beautiful image? The why of a poem can relate to the theme of the poem—the purpose or the main idea.*
- *Why does knowing the "why" of the poem matter? How does knowing the why of the poem help us understand its message?*

How?

- *How is the poem made? What is the poetic structure of the poem?*
- *Does it use figurative language?*
- *Is it free verse?*
- *Does it have rhymes and a rhyme scheme?*
- *What tools did the poet use?*
- *Why does knowing the how of the poem matter? How does knowing the "how" of the poem help us understand its message?*

What If?

Sometimes imagining a different point of view, or a different version of the events of a poem, can help enlighten its meaning.

At the right is an example of a 5W and H Thinking Map for "Ducks on a Winter's Night."

Finding the Theme of a Poem

Finally, gathering all we've learned, what's the theme or message of the poem?

Name: _____   Date: _____

5W and H Thinking Map

Title: *Ducks on a Winter's Night*   Author: *Georgia Heard*

WHO?	WHAT?
· speaker or person named in poem · point of view · tone · speaker's voice *invisible speaker* *3rd person point of view*	· What's happening in the poem? · Does the poem express a feeling, action, observation, thought, etc.? *Ducks are sleeping on a winter's night. They tuck their bills into their feathers to keep warm.*
WHERE?	WHEN?
· Where does the poem or its events take place? *by the banks of a pond*	· When does the poem or its events take place? *on a winter's night*
WHY?	HOW?
· Why do you think the poet wrote this poem? · What's the purpose of the poem? *Possible: an observation.* *To see the world in a new way.* *Seeing ducks sleeping in a new way.*	· How is the poem made? · What craft tools does the poet use? *Use of figurative language (metaphor): Making their own beds/to keep warm in.* *Lines and line breaks.* *Specific words: feathery quills, banks of the pond*
QUESTIONS	PERSONAL CONNECTIONS
What are quills?	*I cover my nose with the blanket when I go to sleep to keep it warm.*

Poetry Lessons to Meet the Common Core State Standards © 2012 by Georgia Heard, Scholastic Teaching Resources

The theme of a poem can be described in the following ways:

- the main idea
- the poet's message
- the poet's vision
- the purpose of the poem

Theme also refers to the emotion and personal connections we bring to the reading of a poem. One poem can have many different themes, and there is no one "right way" of interpreting a poem, but students should show evidence from the details in the poem, as well as their own personal experiences, to support their interpretation.

Close Reading Strategies

Invite students to reread a poem by encouraging them to engage in what Billy Collins calls "spooling back" rereading activities. In the Living With One Poem for a Week model, these close reading strategies will most likely take place on the second and third days; if you're reading a poem on Poetry Fridays, have students engage in a few of these strategies on Fridays.

Illustrating a Poem

Visualizing a poem, and illustrating that imagery, is a comprehension strategy that I use frequently with students in responding to poetry. I tell them that the purpose of visualizing and drawing the images is not to make a perfect drawing but to make visible the mind pictures and sensory imagery that can help clarify the poem's overall meaning and our understanding of it.

After hearing or reading a poem, ask students to draw pictures of what they see in their minds. They may work together or independently. If the poem summons more than one image, then students can use multiple pages to illustrate them. I remind my students that most of the time our quick drawings will not accurately reflect the richness of a poem's sensory and emotional experience, but drawing will slow our reading down and clarify the poem's images and message.

Use some of the following questions to guide students:

- *Draw the what of the poem. What's happening in the poem?*
- *Is the poem a story, an action, or multiple events?*
- *Is the poem an observation?*
- *Draw the where and the when of the poem. What's the setting? Where does the poem take place? When does the poem take place? What are the details in the poem that tell us the where?*

Students can also draw their own personal associations with the poem. If the poem has a figurative meaning, if there is a central metaphor or simile, they can illustrate the fusion of the literal and the figurative.

After illustrating, students can discuss their drawings with partners and have a conversation about what they think the poet's message is. They can also identify and write down evidence and details—words, phrases, and lines—from the text that prompted the images and then share and discuss their illustrations.

Samples: Illustrating and Interpreting a Poem

In a fifth-grade classroom, students read Joanne Ryder's poem "Enchantment" and drew the imagery they pictured in their minds as a way to interpret the poem. (We did not discuss background knowledge or scaffold vocabulary prior to reading or illustrating it.) Students only

heard the poem read once prior to illustrating, and we had no discussion about it. As expected, every student's illustration was different, and so were their interpretations of the poem.

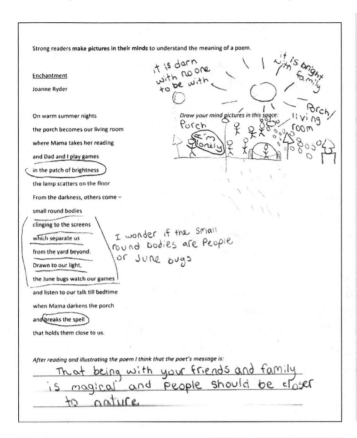

Strong readers **make pictures in their minds** to understand the meaning of a poem.

Enchantment

Joanne Ryder

On warm summer nights

the porch becomes our living room

where Mama takes her reading

and Dad and I play games

in the patch of brightness

the lamp scatters on the floor

From the darkness, others come –

small round bodies

clinging to the screens

which separate us

from the yard beyond.

Drawn to our light,

the June bugs watch our games

and listen to our talk till bedtime

when Mama darkens the porch

and breaks the spell

that holds them close to us.

it is darn with no one to be with

it is bright with family

Draw your mind pictures in this space:

Porch living room

Porch

I'm lonely

I wonder if the small round bodies are people or June bugs

After reading and illustrating the poem I think that the poet's message is:

That being with your friends and family is magical and people should be closer to nature.

Strong readers **make pictures in their minds** to understand the meaning of a poem

Enchantment

Joanne Ryder

On warm summer nights

the porch becomes our living room

where Mama takes her reading

and Dad and I play games

in the patch of brightness

the lamp scatters on the floor.

From the darkness, others come –

small round bodies

clinging to the screens

which separate us

from the yard beyond.

Drawn to our light,

the June bugs watch our games

and listen to our talk till bedtime

when Mama darkens the porch

and breaks the spell

that holds them close to us.

Draw your mind pictures in this space:

this is poetry

After reading and illustrating the poem I think that the poet's message is:

when you spend time with your family it is like almost an enchantment.

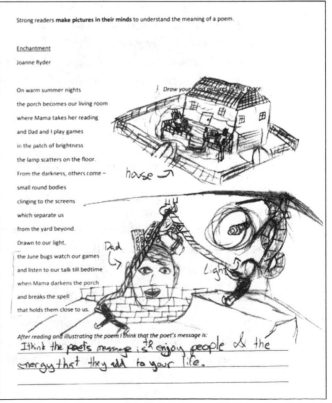

Strong readers **make pictures in their minds** to understand the meaning of a poem.

Enchantment

Joanne Ryder

On warm summer nights

the porch becomes our living room

where Mama takes her reading

and Dad and I play games

in the patch of brightness

the lamp scatters on the floor.

From the darkness, others come –

small round bodies

clinging to the screens

which separate us

from the yard beyond.

Drawn to our light,

the June bugs watch our games

and listen to our talk till bedtime

when Mama darkens the porch

and breaks the spell

that holds them close to us.

Draw your

house

Dad

Light

After reading and illustrating the poem I think that the poet's message is:

I think the poets message is to enjoy people & the energy that they add to your life.

All three of the drawings show an understanding of the details of the poem, and all of their interpretations bring an understanding of the theme of the poem as filtered through the students' personal associations and memories.

All three readers brought their memories and feelings of family into their reading of the poem. I noticed the unusual illustration in the third example—a face, labeled "Dad" with an arrow pointing to it, looking out from a brick wall and a construction site surrounding him. Later, in a conference, the student's teacher helped me understand the drawing. She told me that this student's father had passed away several weeks earlier in a tragic construction accident. I reread this boy's interpretation of the poem, "I think the poet's message is to enjoy people and the energy that they add to your life," and realized that, of course, he read the poem with his dad's life and tragic death in his heart. I understood that when he put brackets around the last five lines of the poem about breaking the spell, it gave the poem a new deeply moving meaning for me.

When we read, we can't help but bring our whole selves and our lives to what we read, and this is precisely what we want our students to do when they read and interpret a poem's meaning.

In a discussion of the poem afterward, I asked students to think about the title "Enchantment" and how it figured in their interpretation. This led to a discussion about what the word *enchantment* referred to: the bugs, the family, or perhaps both. On another day, we also could discuss June bugs, and how and why they're attracted to light and what that means for the interpretation of the poem. Or we could discuss the poet, Joanne Ryder, who also writes informational books about science for children, and how knowing about her as a writer influences our reading of the poem. Or we could discuss the speaker's diction and word choice.

Rereading a poem over several days a week, sometimes even a year, is essential in coming to a complete understanding of it and its theme.

Acting Out a Poem

Performing a poem as a whole class, or in small groups, can help students answer the *what* and *where* of a poem. They can act out the *what* in the poem: *What's going on in the poem? What's the story or action?* They can also act out the *where* of the poem: *Where does the poem take place?* In their performances, students highlight the details of the poem that give us this information.

When they perform, students will need to decide who is going to read the poem aloud as they act it out. After performing, the performers discuss which words and details helped them come to an understanding of how to act the poem out. Some poems are better suited for choral reading than acting out (see the section on choral reading in Chapter 3).

Quick-Writes and Writing About a Poem in Poetry Response Journals

Students can free write a response to the poem in their poetry response journals: they can write how the poem made them feel or what it made them think of. They can write based on a line or an image, or write what they think the poem is about. Writing in response to a poem can also help students understand the why of the poem: *Why do you think the poet wrote the poem? What's the purpose of the poem?*

Rereading a Poem With Different Lenses

In my book *The Revision Toolbox: Teaching Techniques That Work* (2002), I wrote how students sometimes find it helpful as a writing revision strategy to reread their writing using different lenses (such as rereading for clarity, focus, and sound). Similarly, students can also reread a poem with a specific lens to clarify their understanding of it. They could reread a poem with a different lens Monday through Friday, independently or in small groups, and then report back to the class what they learned about the poem.

First, you need to model reading a poem with a particular lens; you can't expect students to understand how to read with, for example, the craft lens if they know nothing about the craft of poetry. Introduce one lens at a time to the whole class Monday through Friday, then model how to read with each lens. Depending on the content and type of poem, you can assign some of these reading lenses.

✳ *Literal Lens*

Students read a poem on the literal level.

- *What does the poem actually say?*
- *What are the concrete and key details?*
- *Can you summarize the poem?*
- *Can you retell the narrative progression of a poem, stanza by stanza?*

✳ *Figurative Lens*

As students read, they ask themselves if the poem has another meaning beside the literal.

- *Does the poem use figurative language, such as metaphors or similes?*
- *Is the poem an extended metaphor, or does it use several similes and metaphors?*
- *Which parts of the poem are similes and which parts are metaphors? What is being compared?*

✳ *Sound Lens*

Students read a poem with their ears. In other words, they read a poem by listening to the sounds and music: rhythm, repetition, rhyme, alliteration, or other sound patterns.

- *What's the rhythm of the poem? Does it change anywhere in the poem? Why?*
- *Does the poem use any sound patterns (such as repetition or alliteration)?*
- *Is there a rhyme scheme?*
- *Does the poem have a set meter or rhythm?*
- *How do the sounds of the poem reinforce the sense or the meaning?*

✳ *Sensory Imagery Lens*

Students read a poem, paying particular attention to the imagery and the sensory words.

- *What mind pictures do you see?* (Students can highlight any words, phrases, and lines that use sensory images or express a feeling. They can draw their mind pictures next to the poem.)
- *Are there any places in the poem where the imagery is not clear because it seems murky or abstract?*
- *Which words, phrases, or lines make you see, taste, touch, hear, and smell?*

✳ *Personal Connection Lens*

Students read a poem, paying attention to which feelings, memories, and thoughts the poem evokes.

✽ Theme Lens

Students read a poem with the lens of finding its theme. One strategy to help students find the theme is to supply one keyword or possible theme and ask them to read the poem with the keyword in mind. The following are some common themes of poems: *courage, beauty, strength, love*. Students can then come up with their own keyword by which to read a poem.

✽ Craft Lens

Students read a poem with the lens of craft.

- *How did the poet construct the poem?*
- *How do these craft tools help convey the poem's message?* (See the list of craft tools below).

✽ Compare-and-Contrast Lens

Students read two poems, or a poem and another text such as a nonfiction text, on the same topic and compare and contrast structure, content, and theme.

✽ Historical Lens

Students read a poem and apply their knowledge of the historical time and events taking place when the poem was written or the time the poet lived.

- *How does historical knowledge give you insights into the poem?*

Thursday: How Does the Poem Say It?

On Thursday, students discuss the how of the poem: *How is the poem built? What is its poetic structure? Is the poem free verse? Is the poem written in meter or rhyming pattern? What are the craft tools the poet uses to bring the meaning of the poem to us?* In the English Language Arts Reading: Literature CCSS, the Craft and Structure section includes a toolbox of poetic devices students are required to know, such as rhythm, rhyme, meter, and stanzas.

Below is a list of some poetic devices poets use to build a poem, many of which I will explain in more detail in later chapters.

- Figurative language (Chapters 6, 7)
- Metaphor (Chapter 7)
- Simile (Chapter 7)
- Imagery (Chapters 4, 6, 7)
- Sensory words (Chapter 4)
- Feeling words (Chapter 4)
- Lines (Verse) and line breaks (Chapters 9, 10)
- Stanzas and stanza breaks (Chapter 9)
- Personification (Chapter 7)
- Point of View
- Rhythm (Chapter 5)
- Rhyme (Chapter 5)
- Meter (Chapter 10)
- Alliteration (Chapter 5)
- Repetition (Chapter 5)
- Genre of poetry: lyric, narrative, dramatic (Chapter 13)
- Formal Poetry: limerick, haiku, blank verse, and so on
- Punctuation

As you discuss these poetic devices, explore the question, *How does this poetic tool help express the meaning and experience of the poem?*

Guided Craft Question Sheet

Students can use the Guided Craft Question Sheet to guide their thinking of the how of the poem. After reading a poem, students choose one or several craft questions to answer and write their thoughts on sticky notes, as well as on the poem, and attach the notes to the appropriate box.

After working independently or collaborating with a partner, group, or entire class, students come together to share, compare, and discuss their craft findings. Support for this larger discussion of the poem comes from their notes and completed Guided Craft Question Sheet.

Once students have identified several key craft tools in a poem, we must guide them to a deeper understanding of how craft supports and adds to a poem's meaning. I always tell my students that craft is at the service of the heart—meaning that the purpose of all the poetic devices and craft in a poem is to help the poet express his or her feelings, experiences, and observations.

Using the Guided Craft Question Sheet will help students get into the habit of writing down the evidence of their growing knowledge of the craft of poetry—and will help you in assessing their knowledge and understanding of poetic craft.

Friday: Who Is the Poet?

Understanding a poet's life may give students insight into the why of the poem. Sometimes it's helpful to know something about the poet, about his or her life, about the time or era in which he or she lived.

Discuss the poet's key biographical information, or read quotes by the poet to see if knowledge of his or her life or process can deepen students' understanding of the poem. Encourage students to ask themselves how the poet's life experiences inspired or affected his or her poetry. Most poets have their own Web sites that give information about their lives.

Gather several poems by the same poet. Ask students to notice what they recognize about the poet's subject matter, style, or craft choices.

- *Does the poet always write about or locate the poem in the natural world?*
- *Does the poet write about similar themes in other poems?*
- *Does the poet always rhyme?*

Putting It All Together

After five days of living with a poem, be sure to leave time for the whole class to discuss their thoughts and explorations. You may want to ask students:

- how they feel about the poem now as compared to when they first read or heard it.
- how their understanding of the poem has changed over the five days.
- what they now think the theme or main idea of the poem is as compared to when they first heard or read it.
- whether they would like to read more poems by the same poet.

Finally, to help you assess your teaching, ask students to identify what as most helpful in growing their understanding of the poem.

The point of living with a poem for five days is to slow down the reading of a poem and to model a variety of strategies that will help students in reading any text critically. After

modeling living with a poem for five days with several poems, you might try asking students to read a poem closely using some of the strategies they've learned to see which strategies they've internalized. Also, you'll want to increase the complexity of the poems as students begin to understand how to closely read a poem.

Having Conversations to Grow Ideas

To build a foundation for college and career readiness, students must have ample opportunities to take part in a variety of rich, structured conversations—as part of a whole class, in small groups, and with a partner. (College and Career Readiness Anchor Standards for Speaking and Listening)

Most of us who are in a book club understand that reading is social. It's natural and enjoyable to want to talk with other people about our reading, and it also helps us grow our ideas about a book.

Our first reading of a poem may be private, but having discussions about it is one of the best ways of deepening our understanding of it. Research shows that having engaged conversations with peers improved standardized test scores no matter what students' reading levels were. In the CCSS, students are required to demonstrate a range of interactive oral connections, including working collaboratively, sharing findings, and listening carefully to others' ideas. To accomplish this in your classroom, pair each student with a partner with whom they will develop their ideas before, during, and after reading. Encourage readers to talk about their interpretations; this will require them to go back to the text for support of their explanations and to attend to words or phrases brought up by others. In this way, interpretations can grow through social interactions. It's important to give students time to talk and reflect on their learning with the whole class, a partner, and in small groups. The conversation time can be brief and may be introduced as a regular part of your reading workshop routine.

Begin with a focused discussion about the poem. Ask partners to think about something specific, to compare mental or written notes, and then have them share their thoughts and responses with the whole class. Model how to use open comments such as the following to unfold a poem:

- *I noticed . . .*
- *It made me think of . . .*
- *What I didn't understand . . .*
- *It reminds me of . . .*
- *It made me feel . . .*

Students can express their responses in the following ways:

- Share understandings
- Share details of the poem that stand out or answer a specific question
- Share what they envisioned
- Ask questions
- Share parts or words they don't understand
- Share observations about craft and poetic structure
- Share memorable words, lines, or parts
- Share ideas when reading a poem with a particular lens

Make sure the discussion remains grounded in the text as much as possible. You can model what a productive conversation looks like through modeling in a fishbowl, whereby you have a conversation with a student while the rest of the class observes, and by modeling your own conversation about a poem with students.

Poetry Response Journals

Keeping poetry response journals is another way students can record their thoughts, images, reflections, questions, quotes, writing, and drawings about poems that they listen to or read independently. In the CCSS, students are required to demonstrate the connection between reading and writing by gathering evidence about what they read and analyzing and presenting that evidence in writing.

Encourage students to use their poetry response journals in the following ways:

- Collect words, phrases, and lines of a poem that are memorable
- Collect key details and lines
- Express feelings evoked by the poem
- Ask questions
- Explicate the meaning of the poem

- Record personal connections and associations
- Draw the imagery
- Write their own original poems inspired by the poems they read
- Collect examples of exemplary craft

Assessment and Evidence of Growing an Understanding of Poetry

How can we measure students' understanding and knowledge of a poem? How can we measure students' knowledge of the poetry component of the CCSS? We can use our observations during one-on-one reading conferences and small- and whole-group discussions, as well as evaluations before and after reading a poem.

When we assess students' knowledge and understanding of a poem, we must keep in mind a few criteria to put our assessment in context:

- *Is the poem engaging and relevant to the student?*
- *Is the complexity of the text appropriate for the student?*
- *How much knowledge of the genre of poetry does the student have?*
- *How much experience does the student have with poetry?*

We also need to take into account the poetic knowledge and skills that the CCSS requires students to know. Again, to help prepare students for the next grade, teachers must be knowledgeable about which standards come before and after their grade level.

Chapters 3–11, the Collaborative Engagement and Independent Application sections, offer activities that will help students practice and further clarify CCSS expectations. These activities mirror the performance tasks that follow the exemplar poems in Appendix B of the CCSS.

In addition to these practices, you should use your written and anecdotal observations to assess students. Note when they show an interest in reading poetry. Show students a poem, picture book, and informational text, and ask them to identify the genre of each text. These observations will also provide valuable feedback to students about their learning. Also prepare summative assessments, such as the one shown on the next page, to assess students' knowledge and understanding of poetry.

A Sample Fourth-Grade Assessment

Prior to reading any poems or discussing any poetry, fourth graders were given "We Are Trees" to read and then were asked to answer a few open-ended questions. The poem is not particularly complex, but its deeper meaning is based on the understanding of a central metaphor.

After reading the poem, the fourth graders were given a Poetry Reading Pre-Assessment Sheet (p. 118) that contained the following questions:

- *What makes this a poem?*
- *What is this poem about? What is the poet's message (big idea)?*
- *What tools do you notice the poet is using to show his or her message?*

In the beginning of the year, prior to reading poetry, many of the students understood the poem only on a literal level and knew nothing about poetic structure and craft. The Poetry Reading Pre-Assessment Sheet below (left) shows one student's response.

But after one month of reading a wide range of poetry and interpreting and discussing the meaning as well as the structural and craft elements of poems, students were asked to read "We Are Trees" again. In the second reading, not only did they understand the figurative meaning of the poem, but now they could also describe its craft elements. Compare the student's second Poetry Reading Assessment Sheet below (right) to his first one; he shows that he has come to completely understand the meaning of the poem.

> **:: We Are Trees ::**
> *by Francisco X. Alarcón*
>
> our roots
> connect
>
> with the roots
> of other trees
>
> our branches
> grow wanting
>
> to reach out
> to other branches

Poetry Reading Pre-Assessment

Read the poem carefully several times, then answer these questions as thoughtfully as you can.

What makes this a poem?

?

What is this poem about? What is the poet's message (big idea)?

That all trees are connected
This poem is about trees.

What tools do you notice the poet using to help show his/her message?

Big Spaces!

We are trees

Poetry Reading Pre-Assessment

Read the poem carefully several times, then answer these questions as thoughtfully as you can.

What makes this a poem?

Ths poem is different from a prose because of its stanzas and line brakes.

What is this poem about? What is the poet's message (big idea)?

I think that Francisco X. Alarcón is trying to say that like trees we are all together thant our roots connect, that we reach out to eachother.

What tools do you notice the poet using to help show his/her message?

I see a medephor and it's that we are trees, I see rythm to lines per stanza and rythm always egual, and I see conicnece with roots branches tree.

CHAPTER 3

Poetry and Fluency

As a graduate student, I was lucky enough to study poetry with the eminent poet Stanley Kunitz. When he read his poems out loud, it sounded like he was singing. His poems were melodic, and he infused every word with feeling. As he read, auditoriums filled with eager listeners would be so riveted that you could hear a pin drop.

A true fluent reading of a poem calls for much more than speed. Fluency is more than getting all the words right. Reading a poem fluently is about recognizing and interpreting the music and the meaning of the language. It's also being able to read expressively and with understanding. In an interview about his wonderful book *The Art of Slow Reading* (2011), Thomas Newkirk writes, "I think it's finding the kind of pace where you feel like you're totally engaged with the reading." A fluent reading is also about loving a particular poem and expressing that passion as we read aloud.

Recognizing signals in a poem and attending to the meaning through tone, mood, pacing, words, and the intentions of the poet is what fluency is all about. That recognition can lead readers toward greater confidence, greater control over written language, and more effective, efficient, and fluent reading.

Reading poetry is a perfect opportunity for readers to practice reading fluently.

How Poetry Supports Fluency

Poetry helps support fluency because it is:

- short, less dense, and therefore more manageable and less intimidating, especially for struggling or reluctant readers.
- engaging, and therefore motivating to read repeatedly.
- chunked in lines and stanzas with white space surrounding the words, so it's easier to read and slows the reader down.
- organized in a structure such as rhyme, rhythm, and repetition.

Many poems are perfect for fluency practice. Research shows that through repeated

readings of a text, the reader experiences improvement in sight word vocabulary and the ability to decode words quickly and accurately, which fosters comprehension.

Ways to Support Fluency Through Poetry

- Do a choral reading of a poem.
- Read poems aloud to model fluent reading (CCSS Appendix B contains read-aloud poetry exemplar texts for grades K–1 and 2–3).
- Create a shared poem experience.
- Read and reread a poem or part of a poem for Readers Theater.
- Interpret a poem's signals as to how it should be read.
- Memorize and recite a favorite poem.

Choral Reading

Choral reading is an interpretative reading by a group of voices. Students may read individual lines or stanzas alone, in pairs, or in unison. True learning comes from the process of figuring out the meaning of the poem and *how* to read and perform it so as to reflect that meaning.

WHY CHORAL READING IS IMPORTANT

This process:

- builds students' confidence as readers.
- motivates students to read.
- provides a model for fluent reading as students listen to other voices reading and can follow along.
- improves the ability to read sight words.
- provides support for struggling or reluctant readers before they read on their own.

How to Introduce Choral Reading

To introduce students to choral reading, begin by choosing a poem that works well for reading as a group. Look for poems that are patterned or predictable and that use repetition, rhyme, or rhythm, and that have two or three different voices built into them.

Provide each student with a copy of the poem or display it on a SMART Board or an overhead projector so students can follow along. Read the poem aloud to model fluent reading. Then ask students to follow along as they join you in reading the poem. Reread it, then have students read the poem in unison. Discuss and/or divide the class into small groups so that the poem may be read aloud by different voices.

Choral Reading Arrangements

You can use the following arrangements for choral reading:

- *Unison Reading:* The whole class reads the poem in unison.
- *Echo Reading:* The leader reads each line, and the group then repeats the line.
- *Leader and Chorus Reading:* The leader reads the main part of the poem, and the group reads the refrain or chorus in unison.

- *Cumulative Reading:* One student or group reads the first line or stanza, and then another student or group joins in as each line or stanza is read.
- *Round Reading:* Divide the class into three groups that read the poem as a round.
- *Word Effect Reading:* As the whole class reads the poem aloud, a small group whispers key words or key lines of the poem.

Poems for Reading Aloud and Choral Reading

The short list poem "Sound of Water" by Mary O'Neill is easy to comprehend and perfect for reading aloud and for choral reading.

    After reading the poem aloud, ask students to follow along. Then try several of the following ways to chorally read the poem:

- The class reads the poem in unison.
- Divide the class into two groups. Both groups read the title and the first line in unison. Then the first group reads the poem from top to bottom, and the second group reads the poem from bottom to top—keeping in sync with the rhythm of the poem and finishing at the same time.
- A small group of students whispers repeatedly "the sound of water" while the rest of the class reads the poem in unison.
- Students read the title and first line in unison and then individual students take turns reading subsequent words.
- After reading the title and first line, students highlight the rhyming words as a class, or independently. Divide the class into two groups. One groups says the words that rhyme, and the second group reads the other words.
- Students can discuss some of the words Mary O'Neill uses to describe the sound of water and then brainstorm more words to add to the poem, or write a new poem that describes the sound of water.

    An excellent type of poem for choral reading is a poem for two voices. The choral arrangement of this type of poem is built into the way it is written on the page. My poem, "My Horse and I," on the next page is an example of a poem for two voices. Here are some ways to use it as a choral reading:

- The whole class reads the poem in unison. (Boys reading the poem can change the word *girl* to *boy*.)
- Divide the class into two groups. Have the first group read the words on the left and the second group read the words on the right. Ask both groups to read the words in bold together.
- Students can read the poem with partners

> **:: Sound of Water ::**
>
> *by Mary O'Neill*
>
> The sound of water is
> Rain,
> Lap,
> Fold,
> Slap,
> Gurgle,
> Splash,
> Churn,
> Crash,
> Murmur,
> Pour,
> Ripple,
> Roar,
> Plunge,
> Drip,
> Spout,
> Skip,
> Sprinkle,
> Flow,
> Ice,
> Snow

- One of my favorite books with poems for two voices books is *You Read To Me, I'll Read To You* edited by Mary Ann Hoberman.

After several choral readings of a poem, students can practice rereading it with a partner or in small groups before performing it for the whole class. Then discuss the meaning of the poem with the whole class.

Reading poetry independently, in pairs, and in small groups can strengthen "reading muscles" over time. Poetry, because it is presented in "small doses," reduces the tension that some readers associate with longer and denser texts. In short, poetry can be less intimidating for many young readers.

Students are ready to read poems independently if they have been engaged in group work of swaying to the rhythm of poetry, dancing and clapping and snapping to the beat, and with choral reading the text together as you help them discover the rich language of poetry.

:: My Horse and I ::
A poem for two voices
by Georgia Heard

We gallop

                      We gallop

Together

                      Together

                      Over the hills,

Across the fields

                      Follow the creek

Who is the girl?

                      Who is the horse?

I am the girl.   **I am the horse.**

We gallop

                      We gallop

Together   **Together**

Together   **Together**

How to Read a Poem Aloud

In a recent interview, Jack Prelutsky was asked if he had any advice for reading poetry aloud. Here is what he said:

> *A poem is a living organism, and no two are alike. Most poems (perhaps all poems) are read best when read aloud. There is no one best way to recite a poem, but some ways are better than others. One trick about reciting poetry is to put yourself in the poet's shoes . . . try and imagine what the poet was really trying to say. If the poem has a message that seems to be getting louder, then you should get louder too. If the action in the poem is getting faster, then you should also be faster . . . . It may also help to look in the mirror when you're practicing.*

> —from an interview in Maryann Yin's Galleycat blog at Media Bistro, April 12, 2012

In addition to Jack Prelutsky's advice about putting yourself in the poet's shoes, here are more tips on how to read a poem aloud:

- Before reading aloud, read a poem several times to familiarize yourself with the feeling, words, and pace.
- Read slowly and clearly but be sure to maintain the flow of the poem.

- Your voice should reflect the personality of the poem and not be too dramatic or monotone. White space in a poem is a signal to pause. Despite what our teachers told us in high school and college, readers do pause after lines in a poem and in between stanzas. The pause may not be long, so the reading won't be choppy, but nevertheless, it is a pause. The length of the pause will vary depending on whether the line has a comma or a period, or if the meaning, thought, or image stops at the end of the line or continues onto the next line.
- For inspiration, watch videos of high school students reciting poems for the Poetry Out Loud National Recitation Contest at www.poetryoutloud.org.

Demonstration Lesson

Reading a Poem's Signals

Materials:

- ✓ A poem like "Ode to the Washing Machine" by Rebecca Kai Dotlich (p. 64) or "My People" by Langston Hughes (p. 104) that has clear signals (a display copy and one copy for each pair)
- ✓ Chart paper and marker
- ✓ Red, yellow, and green colored pencils or markers

In one classroom, students played "poetry conductor" to guide us in reading a poem aloud—just as an orchestra conductor guides the musicians in playing music. One student led the class in reading the poem aloud. The class brainstormed signals for the conductor to use to help read the poem. Then I addressed the group.

Poets, we've been talking together about how to read a poem's signals in order to know how to read it out loud. Well, I was thinking about some of the signals that we see every day on the street telling us when to stop and when to slow down. What are some of the signals that we see on the street? There's a red sign for stop, yellow for slow, and green for go.

I was thinking that a poem has signals, too, that tell us how to read it. Sometimes the signals are easy to read, like after every line or line break there is a pause— but sometimes the poem wants us to slow down or lower our voice or read with a particular feeling, and the signals are less obvious.

I'm going to read a poem, and I'd like you to listen carefully to how I read it— especially places where I pause or slow down or stop or speed up.

Let's write some street signals on the poem to show how we should read it.

Here are some of the signals students found:

- Between stanzas, or at stanza breaks, the readers should stop reading and pause: Students drew red stop signs where the reader should stop reading and pause in the text to show this.
- Between the title and the first line, the reader should pause: Students drew a red stop sign here.
- After every line, or at the line break, the reader pauses: Students drew yellow yield signs.
- Students knew to pay attention to punctuation: A period or a comma at the end of a line adds an extra second of pause, so they added yield signs after these types of punctuation.

- Students created speed limit signs as they listened and decided if there were any parts of the poem that should be read faster or slower.

- Students drew up and down arrows as they listened to the parts in the poem where their voices were louder and softer.

- As they listened to the tone of the poem, students drew emoticons to designate a feeling the poem expressed and where the reader should express an emotion in his or her voice.

You can also choose a "poetry conductor" to use hand signals to lead the class in reading a poem out loud. After the lesson, I asked students to work with reading partners to find the signals of how to read other poems I had given them.

Collaborative Engagement and Independent Application

How do you know when a student is reading fluently? Take notes throughout the year, record and observe students as they work in small groups or independently and as they perform a poem for the class. The following activities will give you plenty of opportunities for assessing your students' fluency.

Performing a Poem

Ask students to choose a favorite poem and give a reading to the class. They can first show you how they marked the poem's signals for reading it aloud. Students' reading should reflect an understanding of fluency. Look for the following aspects of fluency in their performances:

- The meaning, mood, and feeling of the poem are accurately conveyed.
- The poem's signals, such as line breaks and stanza breaks, are heeded.
- Nuances in meaning and feeling are portrayed.
- Musical aspects, such as rhyme, alliteration and rhythm, are addressed.

Finding Reading Signals in a Poem

Have students work with partners and read a poem together, listening for places where their voices pause or stop, go up or down, or get louder or softer. They can then create their own street signals and draw the signals with colored pencils to show their interpretation of how the poem should be read. Students then read the poems aloud to the class.

Giving a Monotone and a Lively Reading of a Poem

Ask students to give two readings of a poem: the first reading should be in a monotone voice as if they're bored, and the second reading should show the nuances and emotions of a fluent reading.

Memorizing a Favorite Poem

As students independently listen to and read poems on Poetry Fridays and on other days, encourage them to choose a poem that they love and want to memorize. Then have them mark the signals of how to read the poem aloud and recite it to the class. (See also the section on memorizing poetry on the next page.)

Making Recordings of Favorite Poems

One of the English Language Arts Standards for Speaking and Listening asks that students create audio recordings of reading poems, and this activity addresses that standard.

As a class, or in small groups, let students listen to recordings of poets reading their work. (You can find poets reading on YouTube, and many poets have their own Web sites.) Students can then choose a favorite poem and practice reading it out loud—marking the poem's signals. They then record these poems on audiotape or make podcasts or videos of them. (See the Favorite Poem Project: www.favoritepoem.org.)

One wonderful teacher I worked with asked her students to illustrate a favorite poem. She then asked them to practice reading their poems aloud. As a video project, she and her students slowly panned a camera over the drawings as the illustrator read the poem aloud. It was a beautiful way to combine technology with reading aloud, as well as including a visual display to support the meaning of the poem.

Turning a Poem into Readers Theater

Have small groups of students choose a favorite poem and create a readers theater of it—rereading the poem several times in the process—and reciting it to the class as part of the performance.

MEMORIZING POETRY

My son had a wonderful teacher in fifth grade who taught students to love reading poetry. Every week, she read a new poem aloud and discussed it line-by-line; students memorized the poems and then recited them in class every Friday. Initially, I was skeptical; I thought this much of a focus would turn my son off to poetry. The poems were difficult, complex, and "old-fashioned" (e.g., "The Charge of the Light Brigade" by Alfred Tennyson; "I Wandered Lonely as a Cloud" by William Wordsworth) but wonderful, complex, and memorable because they were arranged with a metrical rhythm and usually rhymed.

One afternoon I was driving my son and his friends to a school football game, and all the boys in the backseat started to recite "The Charge of the Light Brigade" in unison. In this context, going to a football game, it seemed perfectly apropos. I was so grateful to my son's teacher for giving him the opportunity to know poems he never would have read on his own.

Memorizing a poem is committing a poem to your heart; deciding that the words of the poem are so special that you want to keep it with you always. Mary Ann Hoberman writes about this in her book *Forget-Me-Nots: Poems to Learn by Heart* (2012):

"When you learn a poem by heart," she writes, "it becomes a part of you. You know it in your mind, in your mouth, in your ears, in your whole body. And best of all, you know it forever."

Introduction to Craft and Structure Anchor Standard 4

I heard a story recently on NPR about a 3-year-old boy who was able to recite Billy Collins's poem "Litany" by heart, expressively and fluently. Since the day he was born, the boy's parents said, they had read poems and stories to him, and he had fallen particularly in love with "Litany." When Collins heard about this, it prompted him to contact the boy. They met, and the boy recited the poem to Collins. The videotape of his recitation was posted on YouTube and has received hundreds of thousands of hits, far more hits than Collins's own reading of his poem!

One of the questions people asked the boy's parents was whether the boy really understood what the poem meant or whether he was just reciting it. His mother didn't answer the question directly but instead answered wisely: "He loves words. He loves saying them and hearing them in many different forms."

Young children share a love of words and language with poets and other writers. We spend our lives learning the skill of using words well. With more than one million words in the English language, it's a full-time job.

Ask any writer what the most essential writing craft tool is, and most will say "words." This CCSS Reading Standards for Literature K–5 under Craft and Structure focus on a variety of poetic devices relating to language from kindergarten through grade 5. The chart on the next page lists expectations for kindergarten through fifth grade. I've boldfaced specific parts that refer to poetry or common poetic elements.

Reading Standards for Literature K–5:
Craft and Structure Standard 4

Kindergarten	Grade 1	Grade 2	Grade 3	Grade 4	Grade 5
RL K.4 Ask and answer questions about unknown words in a text.	RL 1.4 **Identify words and phrases in** stories or **poems that suggest feelings or appeal to the senses.**	RL 2.4 **Describe how words and phrases (e.g., regular beats, alliteration, rhymes, repeated lines) supply rhythm and meaning in a** story, **poem** or song.	RL 3.4 **Determine the meaning of words and phrases as they are used in a text, distinguishing literal from nonliteral language.**	RL 4.4 Determine the meaning of words and phrases as they are used in a text, including those that allude to significant characters found in mythology (e.g., Herculean).	RL 5.4 **Determine the meaning of words and phrases as they are used in a text, including figurative language** such as **metaphors and similes.**

(Because poetry is not specifically named in kindergarten and grade 4, I have not written chapters for those grades. Chapters 4–7 focus on grades 1–3 and 5.)

Word Awareness for All Grades

As an introduction to the study of poetry, we can nurture what I call "word awareness" in our classrooms. Word awareness means a growing understanding of the power, variety, and playfulness of words. Word awareness means helping students to become curious and passionate about language and about unknown words, helping them learn to savor words that give them a mental picture, to discover precise and unusual words, and even to know how the parts of speech work.

Wonderful Word Wall

One way to foster word awareness is to create a Wonderful Word Wall, not for the purpose of spelling but to highlight wonderful words such as the following kinds:

- Words that students wonder about and want to know the meaning or origin of
- Words they love the sounds of
- Words that are surprising and show unusual and extraordinary ways of expressing meaning
- Unique ways an author or poet expresses or describes something

- Sensory words
- Feeling words
- Color words

Word Awareness in Read-Alouds, Shared Reading, and Independent Reading

As you're reading aloud in any genre, stop and savor golden or memorable words, a phrase or sentence that you think is an extraordinary description or expression of something. Write any memorable words you find on sentence strips and display them on the Word Wall.

Encourage students to do the same when they read independently. Give them sticky notes so they can write words that stand out and ask them to share on the Word Wall any words they don't understand.

Invite students to collect favorite words in their poetry response journals for use in future writing.

The following chapters on Craft and Structure Anchor Standard 4 provide grade-specific demonstration lessons and performance tasks on a variety of word tools—but every reader of poetry should be familiar with each one of these essential tools.

CHAPTER 4

Craft and Structure Anchor Standard 4 in First Grade

CCSS RL 1.4

Identify words and phrases in stories or poems that suggest feelings or appeal to the senses.

A first-grade poet once said to me, "It's easy to say inside but hard to say outside." Every writer struggles with this. All of us store memories, feelings, and experiences in our minds and hearts, and trying to translate these into words so the reader can experience them is the biggest challenge for writers young and old. Most writers stay away from abstract words—words that don't give readers sensory details or pictures in our minds—and instead choose words that make us smell, taste, see, touch, and hear words that evoke the senses and help the reader create mind pictures.

Anton Chekhov advised other writers, "Don't tell me the moon is shining; show me the glint of light on broken glass." Sensory words make writing come alive.

This standard asks students to begin to identify words that appeal to the senses as an introduction to imagery and figurative language, which they will learn in later grades.

Let me preface this discussion with a caveat: No writer ever sits down and says to himself or herself, "Today I'm going to be using my five senses to write." Most writers, and poets, use sensory **imagery** and language because it's how we experience and remember the world, and it's the most effective way to convey feelings and experiences to our readers.

Five Senses Word Wall

In order for students to become familiar with the sensory vocabulary and imagery used in all genres, create a Five Senses Word Wall to display sensory words from poems, stories, and other texts.

You can also provide opportunities for students to brainstorm lists of sensory words; for example, color words, taste words, touch words, hearing words, sight words, and smell words from read-alouds of all genres.

Sensory Word Lists

Color Words: Red	Taste Words	Touch Words	Hearing Words	Sight Words	Smell Words
cherry	sour	soft	roar	bright	sweet
pink	sweet	rough	hiss	shimmering	perfumed
ruby	crunchy	bumpy	squeak	glistening	fishy

Collaborative Engagement: Shared Five-Sense Poem

To help build students' sensory vocabulary, provide hands-on opportunities and activities like the ones discussed below to help them explore their senses. In these activities, children brainstorm lists of sense words and use the words to write collaborative poems.

Hearing

Gather a variety of materials that make sounds, such as the following:

- sandpaper blocks
- pots and pans
- stones
- keys
- aluminum pie plates
- spoons
- dried beans in a jar

Have children work in small groups, or as a whole class, and explore making sounds with various materials. Ask the entire class to describe the sounds everyone heard and write the words they come up with on the Five Senses Word Wall.

Create a shared poem from these sound words. At the right is a collaborative poem first graders wrote from words generated by pots and pan lids.

A poem like this one provides a natural opportunity to talk about **onomatopoeia** (words that sound exactly like what they mean).

Smell

Create several smell jars. Take five or six small jars and put scented items and liquids, such as the following, inside:

- peppermint flavoring
- lemon rind
- almond extract
- vanilla extract
- orange rind

> :: **Kitchen Band** ::
>
> Bang
>
> Clang
>
> Ping
>
> Ring
>
> Pots
>
> Pans
>
> LOUD!
>
> CRASH!

Have small groups or the whole class take turns exploring the smell jars and then brainstorm words to describe the smells.

You can also discuss the different smells around school and at home: bus fumes, freshly mown grass, leaves, garbage, and so on, and then create a poem from these words and use them to create a collaborative smell poem, like "Things I Smell . . ."

Smell Words
Sweet
Lemony
Sour

Smells Around Us	Smells Around Us
Bus fumes . . .	Motor smell
Leaves . . .	Earthy
Freshly mown grass . . .	Sweet

For the last line of "Things I Smell . . . ," students can add examples of their favorite smells, for example:

- Bacon cooking in the morning
- Dog's fur
- The ocean

Taste

Collect pictures of different foods: ice cream, bread, apples, and so on. Ask children to brainstorm taste words to accompany the pictures. Post this list on the Five Senses Word Wall. Note the types of words and phrases students use to describe different tastes.

Then bring in several kinds of fruit—apples, lemons, oranges, grapes—and ask children to taste each and come up with taste words. If students use words like *good* or *yummy*, model specific words. Then create a class poem about one of the fruits, like the one shown below, which was written with kindergarten students after tasting lemons:

> :: **Things I Smell . . .** ::
>
> Bus fumes leave a motor smell.
> Leaves smell earthy.
> Freshly mown grass smells sweet.
> The best smell of all is:
> My mom's chocolate chip cookies.

Taste Words	
Lemon:	sour, bitter
Banana:	sweet
Apple:	tangy

> :: **Lemons** ::
> Sour
> Juicy
> Zesty
> Bitter
> Makes my mouth hurt!

Touch

Bring in textured objects that children can touch:

- sandpaper
- cotton balls
- fleece
- paper
- pinecone
- stone

Touch Words
Soft
Rough
Jagged
Pointy
Sharp

:: My Dog's Fur ::

Soft
Fuzzy
Silky
Velvety
When I kiss him
It tickles my face!

Ask students to touch each object and brainstorm touch words, develop a Touch Words chart, and then create a shared poem from the words on the chart, or on a personal topic like dog's fur or the bark of a tree.

Sight

Collect souvenirs from nature such as a shell, a bird's nest, an acorn, and so on. Ask students to help you find the words to describe one of the objects. Record their responses in a T-chart like the one shown below. Then look at the same object with a magnifying glass. Let students take a turn, too. Record their new responses. Use the chart to create a shared poem.

Observation: Eyes	Observation: Magnifying Glass
round	ridges
white	swirls
	tiny holes

:: Shell ::

Round
Ridges.
Swirls at the top.
Covered with tiny holes.
I wonder who lives inside?

Keep the objects available at an observation table and encourage students to observe the objects during free time and write their own poems.

Sensory Walks and Writing a Collaborative Sense Poem

In *A Place for Wonder: Reading and Writing Nonfiction in the Primary Grades* (2009), Jen McDonough and I describe a listening walk that children can take around the school. As students walk around outside, they carry clipboards, paper, and pencils. Their job is to listen carefully to what they hear around them: the wind blowing, the rush of traffic, cars honking, birds chirping, and so on. Then they return to the classroom and brainstorm words to describe those sounds. At the right is a poem that a first grader created from a class listening walk.

If going on an outdoor walk is not possible, open your classroom windows and listen to the noises outside.

:: Wind Shhh ::

Shhhh
Wind like an ice cube
Shhhh
Wind strong
Shhhh
Wind like a storm
Shhhh
Wind cool

A good mentor text to pair with this activity is *The Listening Walk* by Paul Showers. This picture book describes a variety of sounds in both suburban and urban settings.

Identifying Words That Appeal to the Senses

Materials:

✓ Poem: "Ears Hear" by Lucia M. Hymes and James L. Hymes, Jr. (display copy)

✓ Chart paper and marker

Display a copy of the poem.

Poets, what I want to talk to you about today are words that poets and all authors use in their writing. Words that, when we close our eyes, we know exactly what that writer is writing about. On our Five Senses Word Wall we have been posting words that use our five senses: taste, touch, sound, sight, and smell.

I'm going to read a poem to you, and I'd like you to listen to the sensory words these poets use. The title of the poem is "Ears Hear."

After reading the poem, have partners share the sound words they heard in it. Ask them to then tell the rest of the class the specific sound words that stood out for them in "Ears Hear."

Collaborative Engagement and Independent Application

Use the following activities to extend and assess learning.

Creating a Shared Poem

With your support, the class creates its own sound poem using "Ears Hear" as a mentor text. First, ask students to name things around school and at home that make noise, such as the school bell, children laughing at recess, trains, cars, and so on. Write their responses on one side of a T-chart, and then on the other side, write down the sound for each suggestion.

:: Ears Hear ::
by Lucia M. Hymes and James L. Hymes, Jr.

Flies buzz,
Motors roar.
Kettles hiss,
People snore.
Dogs bark,
Birds cheep.
Autos honk: Beep! Beep!

Winds sigh,
Shoes squeak.
Trucks honk,
Floors creak.
Whistles toot,
Bells clang.
Doors slam: Bang! Bang!

Kids shout,
Clocks ding.
Babies cry,
Phones ring.
Balls bounce,
Spoons drop.
People scream: Stop! Stop!

Makes Noise	Sound Words
School bell	rinnngggs
Children	laugh: ha ha ha ha
Train	whistles: wooo wooo
Cars	honk

Work with the entire class or small groups to create a poem for two voices from this brainstorm. Add a little twist at the end like the one shown in "Ears Hear" or repeat the first line of the poem as an ending. When the poem is finished, the class can do a choral reading of it. Divide the class into two groups: one group recites the line about the people or things that make the sound, then the second group speaks and performs the sound words.

In most stories and poems that students encounter, the use of sensory words will be more subtle and woven throughout the text. Now that students have become aware of a variety of sensory words, they will be better able to recognize these words in all the genres. Encourage students to write down or highlight sense words as they read or listen to texts in other genres.

:: Ears Hear ::
(Poem for Two Voices)

School bell
　　　Riiiiiiiings
Children
　　　Laugh Ha Ha Ha Ha Ha
Train
　　　Whistles Wooo Wooo
Cars
　　　Honk Honk Honk
QUIET PLEASE!

Acting Out a Poem

Students can act out "Ears Hear" by taking some of the sound words and pairing actions with them. For the line "Flies buzz," for example, one group could say the word "Flies" and the second group could make the sound of the words "buzz bzzzzzz" while they pretend to be flies.

Demonstration Lesson (Day 2)

Identifying Words and Phrases That Appeal to the Senses

Materials:

- ✓ Poem: "Ice Cream Cone" by Heidi E. Y. Stemple
- ✓ Book: *Frederick* by Leo Lionni
- ✓ Reproducible: Five Senses Word Sheet (p. 119)
- ✓ Highlighter

On Day 2, the focus is still on identifying words that appeal to the senses, but the words should be more subtly woven into the text. Display the copy of "Ice Cream Cone."

We've talked a lot these past few days about sense words. I'd like to share another poem that uses sense words. I'll read the poem, and I'd like you to listen carefully for the sensory words that make the poem come alive.

Turn and talk with your reading partner and share the "sense" words you heard in this poem.

:: Ice Cream Cone ::
by Heidi E. Y. Stemple

Strawberry ice cream
cold and sweet;
sugar cone
my favorite treat!

Pink and sticky
melting drips;
lick it off
my finger tips!

Then have partners tell the rest of the class which sense words they heard. Record their responses in a chart, and highlight those words in the poem.

This poem, and many other poems, use sense words. Let's keep listening for words that make us see, hear, touch, taste, and smell, and we'll add these to our Five Senses Word Wall.

Sense Words in "Ice Cream Cone"

Taste Words	Sight Words	Touch Words
cold	pink	sticky
sweet	melting	
lick		

Collaborative Engagement and Independent Application

With the entire class or small groups, read poetry, picture books, and informational texts that use sensory language. Ask students to identify which sensory words help them picture the words. The following poetry books, picture books, and informational books include good examples of sensory images:

- *One Leaf Rides the Wind: A Japanese Counting Book* by Celeste Davidson Mannis
- *Owl Moon* by Jane Yolen
- *Night in the Country* by Cynthia Rylant
- *Bat Loves the Night* by Nicola Davies
- *Outside Your Window: A First Book of Nature* by Nicola Davies
- *Red Sings from Treetops: A Year in Colors* by Joyce Sidman

Completing a Five Senses Word Sheet

After students listen to a text or read it independently, ask them to record the sensory imagery on sticky notes and attach the notes to a Five Senses Word Sheet in the appropriate place.

Illustrating and Recording Sensory Images

Read aloud *Frederick* by Leo Lionni. As you read, ask students to close their eyes and imagine the images that Frederick stores in his mind. Either collaboratively or independently, students can illustrate and write down their favorite *Frederick* sensory images.

Name: _____ Date: _____

Five Senses Word Sheet

Title: _____ Author: _____

Look for sense words, phrases, or lines in the poem. Write them on a sticky note. Place the sticky note in the correct box.

See	Hear
Touch	Taste
Smell	

Poetry Lessons to Meet the Common Core State Standards © 2012 by Georgia Heard, Scholastic Teaching Resources

Other Poems That Use Sensory Words and Imagery

Touch	See	Taste	Hear	Smell
"Cat Kisses" by Bobbi Katz "Coins" by Valerie Worth "Aquarium" by Valerie Worth	"Tiger" by Valerie Worth "Until I Saw the Sea" by Lilian Moore "Laughing Boy" by Richard Wright (in Appendix B K–1 CCSS)	"sweets" by Valerie Worth	"Manhattan Lullaby" by Norma Farber "Wind Song" by Lilian Moore "Scarecrow Complains" by Lilian Moore "Zin! Zin! Zin! a Violin" by Lloyd Moss (in Appendix B K–1 CCSS)	"September" by John Updike

Demonstration Lesson (Day 1)

Identifying Words and Phrases That Suggest Feelings

Materials:

- ✓ Poem: "A Circle of Sun" by Rebecca Kai Dotlich (p. 55)
- ✓ Photos and/or pictures from magazines showing children expressing feelings
- ✓ Chart paper and marker
- ✓ Paper and markers or colored pencils
- ✓ Plain white paper plates

A few years ago, Rita Dove was asked what she would like to accomplish as poet laureate of the United States, and she said, "I would like to remind people that we have an inner life, and that without that inner life we are shells." Poetry is the genre of the inner life.

Emotional self-awareness—being able to recognize feelings and building a vocabulary for those feelings—is an essential foundation for emotional literacy, but it also will help develop readers who can fully empathize as part of their understanding of a text. One of my goals is to nurture empathetic readers for all genres, not just poetry. As you read aloud, or as students read independently, ask which emotions the text makes them experience and to identify some of the words and phrases that make them feel this way. First grade is a good place to start helping children build a feelings vocabulary, and poetry is the ideal genre to begin a discussion about emotions in texts we read. The combination of sensory language and words that suggest feelings helps readers experience writing in a personal and connected way.

Start by creating a classroom chart of feeling words. Show the photos and magazine pictures

to introduce a variety of feeling words, beginning with the primary emotions like happy, mad, sad, and scared, and then gradually add feeling words to expand children's vocabulary.

Feeling Words

Happy	Mad	Sad	Scared
Glad	Angry	Disappointed	Afraid
Bubbly	Upset	Hurt	Worried
Cheerful	Hateful	Lonely	Frightened
Tickled	Grouchy	Unhappy	Trembly
Joyful	Grumpy	Rotten	Anxious
Sparkly	Boiling	Awful	Fearful
Delighted	Cross	Blue	Shaken

Then read aloud a poem and ask students to act it out.

One of the really special qualities about poetry is that it expresses feelings. Sometimes a poem expresses happiness and sometimes sadness—and many other different emotions. When we hear a poem or a story that makes us feel something, we can say, "I feel exactly the same way." Or "I know exactly how that person feels."

I want to read a poem that expresses feelings. This poem is called "A Circle of Sun" by Rebecca Kai Dotlich. (Display a copy of the poem and read it aloud.)

Let's stand up and act this poem out as I read it a second time. (Read each line slowly to give students time to act out the movements.)

What feelings were the words of the poem telling you to act out? That's right, a happy feeling. Let's look at the poem again and highlight the words that give you a happy feeling. (Chart students' responses. A sample chart appears below.)

"Circle of Sun" Happy Words
Giggle
Grin
Funny
Dancing
Singing
Wiggle

:: A Circle of Sun ::
by Rebecca Kai Dotlich

I'm dancing.
I'm leaping.
I'm skipping about.
I gallop.
I grin.
I giggle.
I shout.
I'm Earth's many colors.
I'm morning and night.
I'm honey on toast.
I'm funny.
I'm bright.
I'm swinging.
I'm singing.
I wiggle.
I run.
I'm a piece of the sky
in a circle of sun.

Collaborative Engagement and Independent Application

Use the following activities to extend and assess learning.

Choral Reading

Do a choral reading of "A Circle of Sun." Ask each student, or a pair of students, to read one line. Remind students that they will need to follow along with the poem to hear where their part comes in. You can end the poem by having students join hands to form a circle, and say in unison the last two lines of the poem: "I'm a piece of the sky/in a circle of sun."

Afterward, have a conversation about the title of the poem. Ask students why they think the poem is called "A Circle of Sun" and why the poet uses happy words in it.

Acting Out and Illustrating a Poem

Have a small group act out another poem that expresses a feeling, and focus particular attention on the feelings that the poem expresses. Other students can guess what the feeling is from the performance. Guide the performers in illustrating expressive faces on paper plates to use in acting out the poem; for example, for "A Circle of Sun," the paper-plate illustrations might feature a grinning face, a sun face, or a picture of morning (sun) and night (moon and stars).

Illustrating

Tell students to illustrate the sensory pictures that "A Circle of Sun" summons in their mind. They can either illustrate each image or mind picture on a sheet of paper or create a picture book with multiple illustrations. Be sure to remind students to include the title of the poem in their illustrations.

Shared Writing: Writing a Poem About Being Happy

Ask each student to think of one word that describes how it feels when he or she is happy and create a shared list poem from these happy words.

Demonstration Lesson (Day 2)

Identifying Words and Phrases That Suggest Feelings

Materials:

✓ Poems: "When I Was Lost" by Dorothy Aldis and other poems that suggest feelings (p. 57)

The Day 2 lesson uses a poem that conveys a different feeling from the text in Day 1. Part of using poetry to develop emotional literacy in our students involves offering them a variety of poems that touch upon a range of emotions. Display a copy of "When I Was Lost."

> *I'm going to read another poem that gives the reader a different feeling. See if you can name the feeling in this poem. Do you think the feeling might be based on the title of the poem, "When I Was Lost"?*

:: When I Was Lost ::

by Dorothy Aldis

Underneath my belt
My stomach was a stone.
Sinking was the way I felt.
And hollow.
And Alone.

Turn and talk to your partner about some of those words or phrases you remember the poet using to describe how scared the speaker of the poem felt.

This poem provides students an opportunity to "read between the lines" and may be their first exposure to figurative language. Ask why the poet didn't say, "I was scared" but instead used words that appeal to our senses; for example, "My stomach was a stone/sinking was the way I felt."

Collaborative Engagement and Independent Application

Use the following activities to extend and assess learning.

Illustrating a Feeling

Encourage students to illustrate "When I Was Lost" or a similar personal experience that made them feel scared.

Shared Writing: Writing a Poem About Being Scared

Have students write a shared poem about a time they were scared. First, brainstorm words that describe how they felt at the time. Together, create a shared list poem using students' responses like the one at the right, which I wrote with students.

Identifying Feelings in Poems

During read-alouds and shared reading, ask students to identify the feeling in a poem (see the suggestions below) and try to identify which words or images portray that feeling. Discuss what the feeling of the poem is and then ask students how they were able to identify it.

> **:: Scared! ::**
>
> Heart thumping
> Sweating
> Shivers up my spine
> Goose Bumps
> Shaking
> Knees wobbling
> It's Halloween!

Poems That Express Feelings

Sad	Angry	Scared	Happy
"Moving" by Eileen Spinelli "Since Hanna Moved Away" by Judith Viorst	"Mad Song" by Myra Cohn Livingston "The Bad-Mood Bug" by Brod Bagert "The NO-NO Bird" by Andrew Fusek Peters	"If a Bad Dream Comes" by Siv Cedering Fox	"And My Heart Soars" by Chief Dan George "Mud" by Flanders and Swann "Celebration" by Alonzo Lopez (in Appendix B K–1 CCSS)

Reading Exemplar Poems in CCSS Appendix B

The following poems in CCSS Appendix B (www.corestandards.org/assets/Appendix_B.pdf) feature words and phrases that suggest feelings:

"Celebration" by Alonzo Lopez
"Poem" by Langston Hughes
"Covers" by Nikki Giovanni

"Singing-Time" by Rose Fyleman
"By Myself" by Eloise Greenfield
"Over in the Meadow" by John Langstaff

CHAPTER 5

Craft and Structure Anchor Standard 4 in Second Grade

CCSS RL 2.4

Describe how words and phrases (e.g., regular beats, alliteration, rhymes, repeated lines) supply rhythm and meaning in a story, poem, or song.

Poetry makes us dance, clap our hands, and snap our fingers, just like songs. Music in a poem is a kind of glue that holds a poem together. There are many different kinds of musical tools in poetry: rhyme, rhythm, and repetition, to name a few. Children delight in the playfulness and musicality of poems that rhyme and use word patterns. When we read a poem, we pay attention not only to what the poem means but also to how it sounds.

Donald Hall writes: "I say you read poems with your mouth, not with your ears, and they taste good. When I read a book silently, sitting in my chair, my throat gets tired. My mouth is really working, chewing on these sounds."

Poets use poetic devices from two toolboxes: the sensory word toolbox and the musical toolbox. The sensory toolbox contains poetic devices that give a poem meaning through tools such as imagery and figurative language; the musical toolbox contains poetic devices that give a poem meaning through devices such as rhyme and rhythm.

Standard RL 2.4 focuses on how poets use musical tools to give a poem meaning. By second grade, most children know that some poems rhyme, and they can identify what a rhyme is. They are less familiar with other musical tools that poets use, which are equally important, such as rhythm, regular beats, alliteration, and repeated lines.

The standard for grade 2 doesn't just ask students to *identify*, or understand, how words and phrases (e.g., regular beats, alliteration, rhymes, repeated lines) supply rhythm and meaning to a poem, as it does in the corresponding grade 1 standard. Instead, it asks students to *describe* how such words and phrases (e.g., regular beats, alliteration, rhymes, repeated

SENSORY TOOLBOX: Expressing feelings and experiences through visual and sensory tools	MUSICAL TOOLBOX: Expressing feelings and experiences through rhythmic and other musical tools
Imagery	Rhythm
Metaphor	Meter
Simile	Alliteration
Personification	Rhyme
Sense Words	Repeated Lines

lines) supply rhythm and meaning to a poem. There's a subtle but important difference between identifying and describing. Students in grade 2 are expected not just to label but also to explain their understanding of how words and phrases supply rhythm and meaning in order to begin to explicate a poem orally or in written form. Conversation with peers, and as a class, as well as written responses in poetry response journals become an important part of close reading and describing responses to a poem.

Demonstration Lesson

How Regular Beats Supply Rhythm and Meaning to a Poem

Materials:

✓ Poems: "Eagle Flight" by Georgia Heard (p. 60) (display copy); "Song of the Dolphin" by Georgia Heard (p. 61) (one copy for each student)

✓ Highlighter

✓ Pencils or pens

When I read poetry to children, they sway and nod their heads and snap their fingers to the beat. They know the music of the poem because they feel it in their bodies. How do words do this? Rhythm. *Rhythm* comes from a Greek word *rhythmos* meaning "measure," as in music in which a bar of music has a particular number of beats. Poets use a variety of tools to give a poem rhythm.

One device poets use to give a poem a rhythm—especially traditional poems such as nursery rhymes or formal poetry such as a limerick—is regular beats. Here is how I use my poem "Eagle Flight" to teach a lesson on connecting regular beats to the rhythm and meaning of a poem. After displaying a copy of the poem, I say:

Some poems are like music—they make us want to clap our hands and dance to the words. I'm going to read a poem out loud. As I read, let's clap our hands to its rhythm.

:: Eagle Flight ::

by Georgia Heard

Eagle gliding in the sky,

circling, circling way up high—

wind is whistling through your wings.

You're a graceful kite with no string.

Where you clapped your hands is called the beat of the poem. I'll read the poem again, and this time, let's count the number of times you clap your hands in each line. (After you read each line, write down the number of claps next to it so students can see it and highlight the syllables, or the beat, of the poem. The beats are boldfaced in the poem below.)

Eagle **gliding in** the **sky,**	4 claps
circling, **cir**cling **way** up **high—**	4 claps
wind is **whist**ling **through** your **wings.**	4 claps
You're a **grace**ful **kite** with no **string.**	4 claps

In this poem, each line has four claps or beats. It's interesting to note that the strong syllables give the poem its beat, or rhythm. But we didn't clap our hands at every syllable. We clapped our hands instead at the beat. A beat also happens at key words. (Underline or highlight the part of each word that has a beat.)

Now I'd like you to try it on your own. I'll give you another poem called "Song of the Dolphin," and I'd like you to work with a reading partner, clap your hands to the rhythm of the poem as you read it, write down the number of beats in each line, and then tell your partner if you think the poem uses regular beats and why the poet uses them.

Distribute a copy of "Song of the Dolphin" to each student and ask partners to clap and to count the beats. As you confer with students, notice if they are counting syllables rather than beats. For "Song of the Dolphin," they should be counting four beats to a line, not ten syllables. Listen to conversations to see how students are describing the poem's rhythm and meaning. When you return to the meeting area to share with the entire group, first ask students to share their process of counting regular beats, then deepen the conversation by asking them to describe how these beats add to the meaning of the poem. In one class, a student said, "Beats are like the music of the poem. You don't clap at every word because it would make the poem sound like a robot."

:: Song of the Dolphin ::
by Georgia Heard

I am a **dol**phin. I **swim** in the **sea**,
Flipping and **shin**ing. **Can** you **see** me?
Now you **do**, and **now** you **don't**.
Try and **catch** me—you **won't**, you **won't**!

I **jump** in the **air** and **feel** so **free**,
twisting and **turn**ing. **Can** you **see** me?
Now you **do**, and **now** you **don't**.
Try and **catch** me—you **won't**, you **won't**!

Collaborative Engagement and Independent Application

Use the following activities to extend and assess learning.

Acting Out a Poem

Challenge students to act out the rhythm and meaning of "Song of the Dolphin." Ask them to form a circle and then select one child to be the dolphin. The rest of the class will be the waves that sway back and forth to the rhythm of the poem. As you and the students say the poem aloud, the dolphin swims in and out of the swaying ocean waves. Let students take turns playing the dolphin.

I saw a wonderful teacher perform this poem with her students. She turned the performance into a game of tag, in which the dolphin tags another student after the line, "Try and catch me—you won't, you won't!" and the two darted in and out of the swaying waves.

After the performance, have a conversation about the rhythm in the poem, particularly how it helps give the poem meaning. Explore questions like the following:

- *Why do you think this poem has a strong rhythm?*
- *How does the rhythm add to the meaning of the poem?*
- *Are the rhythms of the ocean and the dolphin swimming in the waves similar to the rhythm of a poem?*

Choral Reading

Divide the class into two groups for a choral reading of "Song of the Dolphin." The first group speaks the first two lines of both stanzas in unison, clapping to the rhythm, and the second group does the same for the last two lines of both stanzas:

First group:

I am a dolphin, I swim in the sea.
Flipping and shining, can you see me?

Second group:

Now you do, and now you don't!
Try and catch me—you won't, you won't!

After the reading, discuss how the rhyming words add rhythm to the poem and how the poet supplied rhythm to it.

Reading Exemplar Poems in CCSS Appendix B, Grades 2–3

From Appendix B (www.corestandards.org/assets/Appendix_B.pdf), choose one of the following poems that uses regular beats:

"Autumn" by Emily Dickinson

"Who Has Seen the Wind" by Christina Rossetti

"Afternoon on a Hill" by Edna St. Vincent Millay

"Something Told the Wild Geese" by Rachel Field

"Stopping by Woods on a Snowy Evening" by Robert Frost

Ask students to do the following as you read aloud the poem:

- Clap their hands to the beat of the poem.
- Count the number of regular beats in each line.
- Notice and discuss how the number of beats changes within the same poem.
- Discuss how regular beats add meaning to the poem.

Demonstration Lesson

Alliteration

Materials:

✓ Poem: "Ode to the Washing Machine" by Rebecca Kai Dotlich (p. 64) (one copy for each student)

✓ Highlighters, pens, or pencils

When I was a girl, my mother read me Mother Goose rhymes. I loved the nonsense words and the rhymes, but I particularly loved alliterative poems:

Peter Piper picked a peck of pickled peppers . . .
and
She sells seashells down by the seashore . . .

On long car rides, my sister and I would recite these poems over and over, faster and faster, as tongue twisters—driving everyone in the car crazy.

Alliteration is like a musical spell; hearing the same initial sounds repeated throughout a

line adds a musical dimension to a poem. Most poems and prose use alliteration sparingly, and its effect is much more subtle than the above tongue twisters, so students have to listen for alliteration carefully as I show in the following example:

> *I read the title of a poem recently that really stood out to me. The title was "Ants, Although Admirable, Are Awfully Aggravating" by Walter R. Brooks.*
>
> *Do you hear all the "A" sounds? The poet is using a technique that all writers use.*
>
> *That technique is called alliteration. Writers sometimes repeat the beginning letter of a word to make a kind of music in the poem.*
>
> *Sometimes writers use alliteration just once or twice in a text, and the reader hardly notices it. Listen to the following line by the poet Robert Frost and see if you can hear any alliteration:*
>
> *"It is a blue-butterfly day here in spring. . . ."*
>
> *Do you hear the two "B" sounds in "blue-butterfly"? Or listen to this line by Rebecca Kai Dotlich:*
>
> *"Here's to your spin; your soapsud song/your rumble and whirl and twirl along"*
>
> *Do you hear the "S," "V," and "R" sounds? That's alliteration.*
>
> *Alliteration is a kind of rhyming—it's repeating the same sound in several words. Alliteration gives the poem a kind of music that makes us enjoy it as we listen to those repeating sounds.*
>
> *Today, I'm going to give you a poem that has alliteration in it. Please work with your reading partner: read the poem together, then go back and highlight the alliteration—the sounds you hear that are repeated, and write the repeated sound next to the lines.*

Distribute a copy of "Ode to the Washing Machine" to each student. Ask partners to read the poem together and then highlight the alliteration and write the repeated sound next to each line. (As you can see, this wonderful poem uses numerous musical tools in addition to alliteration, including rhyme, repetition, rhythm, assonance, and consonance.) Students can also record their favorite lines of alliteration in their poetry response journals.

When you bring the class together to share the alliterations they found, ask students why they think the poet used alliteration and how alliteration adds to the poem's meaning.

Collaborative Engagement and Independent Application

Use the following activities to extend and assess learning.

Using the Sound Lens

Have students read "Ode to the Washing Machine" using the Sound Lens (p. 31). Tell them to identify other musical tools the poem uses (besides alliteration) and discuss how these musical tools add to the meaning of the poem.

:: Ode to the Washing Machine ::
by Rebecca Kai Dotlich

Here's to your **spin**; your **soapsud** <u>song</u>	**s** (alliteration, rhyme)
your **rumble** and whi**r**l and twi**r**l <u>along</u>	**r** (alliteration, rhyme)
swish swish swish	**sw** (repetition)
swirl and <u>spin</u>,	**s** (alliteration, off rhyme)
a **t**ub of **t**umbling safe**t**y <u>pins</u>	**t** (alliteration, off rhyme)
and jeans and <u>socks</u>	**s** (alliteration, off rhyme)
and nickels that **kn**ock	**n** (alliteration, off rhyme)
their silver **s**ong in the whirling drum	**s** (alliteration)
of your belly.	
Twist, **t**ub, *<u>twist</u>*,	**t** (alliteration, repetition, off rhyme)
do the twist,	(pun)
give the **s**ocks a **s**oapy <u>kiss</u>;	**s** (alliteration, off rhyme)
scrub our jeans good and <u>clean</u>,	**s** (alliteration, off rhyme)
yellow the *yellows*, green-up the <u>greens</u>.	(repetition, off rhyme)
Bub bub bubble	**b** (alliteration, repetition)
bubble along . . .	
here's to your **s**pin, your **s**oapsud **s**ong.	**s** (alliteration)

Acting Out a Poem

To highlight the rhythm of the poem, ask students to act out the actions in "Ode to the Washing Machine" as they say the lines.

Shared or Independent Writing: Writing an Alliterative Poem

As a group or independently, students can try writing their own alliterative poem by thinking of one letter to repeat. Remind them that their poem must make sense. At the right is an alliterative poem I wrote using the letter *s*.

Noticing Alliteration in Picture Books

Read aloud a picture book that uses alliteration, such as *Raccoon Tune* by Nancy Shaw or *Big Chickens* by Leslie Helakoski. Ask students to identify places where the author uses alliteration.

:: Summer Snakes ::
by Georgia Heard

Sssssnakes

Sssslither

Sssswiftly

Over Ssssizzling

Sidewalks

Reading Exemplar Poems in CCSS Appendix B

Read one or more of the following poems from the CCSS Appendix B Grades 2–3 Text Exemplars (www.corestandards.org/assets/Appendix_B.pdf) and ask students to search for examples of alliteration:

"Autumn" by Emily Dickinson

"Afternoon on a Hill" by Edna St. Vincent Millay

"Weather" by Eve Merriam (Text of poem does not appear in CCSS Appendix B.)

"Eating While Reading" by Gary Soto

Demonstration Lesson

Rhyme

Materials:

✓ Poem: "Favorite Bear" by Georgia Heard (p. 66) (display copy and 1 copy for each student)

✓ Highlighter

If you ask most students what they think a poem is, they'll usually say it's something that rhymes. Rhyme has become synonymous with poetry. Rhyme is playful, fun, and children love it. We can teach students to spot rhyming words and to recognize rhyming patterns as in this simple nursery rhyme, "Pease Porridge Hot."

Show students how to indicate the rhyming pattern or **rhyme scheme** by using the same lowercase letter of the alphabet for all word patterns that rhyme. The rhyme scheme for "Pease Porridge Hot" then would be *a-b-a-b*, which shows that the rhyming words alternate lines. Poets frequently use alternating rhyming lines so the rhyme scheme doesn't sound too obvious. In most poems, the last word of the line rhymes, which is called an **end rhyme**. A rhyme inside the line is called an **internal rhyme**. Most poets use rhyming words that are **exact rhymes**: *hog* and *log* are exact rhymes, but poets also use slant rhyme (e.g., the final consonants of the words *ill* and *shell* make the pair a **slant rhyme**). The chart on the next page shows some of the varieties of rhyming patterns and types of rhyme.

Pease porridge hot	a
Pease porridge cold	b
Pease porridge in-the-pot	a
Nine days old.	b

In many contemporary poems the rhyme is disguised. Lilian Moore writes that she prefers to "chime" her poems, which means she sprinkles rhyming words intermittently throughout a poem, so the rhyming sound is subtle.

Here's how I introduce rhyme as shown on the next page:

Now that we've listened to a lot of poems, we know that sometimes poems rhyme and sometimes they don't. But not every word in a poem has to rhyme. It's usually the last word in the line that rhymes. I'm going to read a poem called "Favorite Bear." Listen for the words at the end of lines that rhyme and that's called an "end rhyme."

:: Favorite Bear ::

by Georgia Heard

Grizzlies wander the meadows all **day**,	a
searching for squirrels to scamper their **way**.	a
Black bears and brown bears mark the **trees**,	b
clawing the bark, shaking the **leaves**.	b
Polar bears fish in ice and **snow**,	c
with leathery pads and fur between their **toes**.	c
Sun bear has a lighter nose than the **rest**	d
and uses its tongue to lick honey from a **nest**.	d
Although a teddy bear can't do any of these **things**,	e
it's my favorite because of all the hugs it **brings**.	e

Do you hear which words rhyme? Let's highlight them as we read the poem again.

As you read the poem line-by-line, you'll notice that some of the rhyming words are exact rhymes (*rest/nest* and *things/brings*), and some are off, or slant rhymes (*snow/toes* and *trees/leaves*). Have a conversation with your students about these two different kinds of rhyme.

Later, you can also introduce other types of rhymes shown in the chart below.

Rhyming Chart

Type of Rhyme	Definition
Exact or Perfect Rhyme	A repetition of similar sounds with all but the first letter being identical: *hot, pot*
Slant, Imperfect, or Half Rhyme	Rhymes that are close but not exact: *twist, kiss*
Consonance	The repetition of internal or ending consonant sounds in words close together: *litter/batter, dress/boss*
Assonance	The repetition of internal vowel sounds in words close together: I *made* a *cake* today.
End Rhyme	Rhymes that occur at the end of lines
Internal Rhyme	Rhymes that occur within a line

Collaborative Engagement and Independent Application

Use the following activities to extend and assess learning.

Cloze

After reading "Favorite Bear" aloud, cover up several rhyming words and ask students to work with their reading partners to guess what the rhyming words are. Then give each student a copy of the poem, and ask them to discuss the kinds of rhymes it uses.

Clapping to Rhyming Words

As you read "Favorite Bear," or any other rhyming poem, ask students to clap their hands when they hear the rhyming words.

Reading Rhyming Poems Independently

Select other poems that use different rhyming patterns and ask students to identify and highlight the rhyming words. Then ask them the following questions:

- *Why does the poet use rhyming words?*
- *What is the rhyme scheme?*
- *Does the poet use exact or slant rhymes?*
- *Does every end word rhyme?*

Students can write responses in their poetry response journals, or discuss with partners the rhyming patterns of the poems.

Reading Exemplar Poems in CCSS Appendix B

Many poems in CCSS Appendix B Grades 2–3 Text Exemplars (www.corestandards.org/assets/Appendix_B.pdf) rhyme. After discussing some of the following poems, ask students to identify the rhyme in each one:

"Autumn" by Emily Dickinson

"Who Has Seen the Wind?" by Christina Rossetti

"Afternoon on a Hill" by Edna St. Vincent Millay

"A Bat Is Born" by Randall Jarrell

Repeated Lines

Materials:

- ✓ Poems: "Bat Patrol" by Georgia Heard (below) (display copy)

  "A Bat Is Born" by Randall Jarrell (www.corestandards.org/assets/Appendix_B.pdf)

  "Ode to the Washing Machine" by Rebecca Kai Dotlich (p. 64)
- ✓ Book: *Bat Loves the Night* by Nicola Davies
- ✓ Reproducible: Musical Tools Reading Sheet (p. 120)
- ✓ Sticky notes

Repeating lines, words, or phrases is another type of rhyming and a way poets make poems musical. Poets use repetition for a variety of reasons and in a variety of ways, but repetition has the same effect on a poem—it glues the poem musically together. Here are three common repeating line patterns:

1. The first line(s) and last line(s) are repeated.
2. One line or a couple of lines are repeated throughout the poem in a pattern called a **refrain**.
3. The first word or words of two or more lines are repeated.

This is how you might introduce students to repeated lines in poetry:

Some poems sound like songs, and one way that poems are like songs is that they repeat words, lines, and even whole sentences. Listen to this poem, "Bat Patrol." Can you hear the lines that the poet repeats?

:: Bat Patrol ::

by Georgia Heard

Quickly and quietly,

the bat patrols the night,

sending an invisible song

echoing like ripples on a pond,

chasing moths around a streetlight.

Quickly and quietly,

the bat patrols the night.

Poets repeat lines for several different reasons:

- *Sometimes the repeating lines have a special meaning.*
- *Sometimes the repeating lines give the poem a rhythm like a song.*

- *Sometimes the repeating lines give the poem a circular ending—the poem begins and ends with the same line or lines.*

  Let's take a minute and talk about why you think the poet used repeating lines in this poem and how you think repeating lines support the meaning of the poem.

Collaborative Engagement and Independent Application

Use the following activities to extend and assess learning.

Choral Reading

Divide the class into two groups. The first group speaks the two repeating lines (refrain) of "Bat Patrol" in unison, and the second group reads the rest of the poem. Both groups should say the title and the poet's name together. After reading, discuss with students how the repeating lines add meaning to the poem.

Comparing and Contrasting Texts

Here are two options:

- Read aloud "Bat Patrol" and then the information book *Bat Loves the Night* by Nicola Davies. Then have students compare and contrast these texts on the same topic. Ask them to pay particular attention to the use of musical devices in both the information book and the poem.

- Read aloud "A Bat Is Born" by Randall Jarrell. As a class, identify alliteration, rhymes, and repeated lines in the poem and discuss how these musical devices make meaning in the poem. Then compare and contrast content, craft, structure, and theme of the texts "Bat Patrol," *Bat Loves the Night*, and "A Bat Is Born."

Reading Independently

Give students several poems that use musical tools like rhyme, rhythm, alliteration, and repeating lines, such as "Ode to the Washing Machine" by Rebecca Kai Dotlich and my poem "Eagle Flight" and a copy of the Musical Tools Reading Sheet reproducible. Ask students to select one of the poems, identify which musical tools the poem uses, and write examples of them on sticky notes to place on the sheet. As in "Ode to the Washing Machine," some poets use multiple musical tools throughout a poem. After students complete the reproducible, discuss how these musical tools add meaning to the poems.

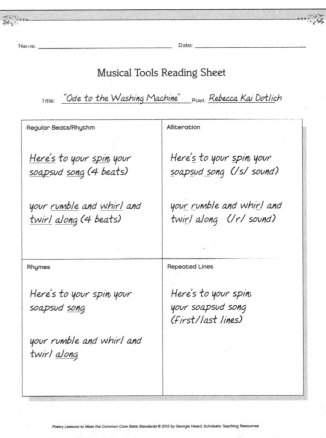

Name: _____ Date: _____

Musical Tools Reading Sheet

Title: *"Ode to the Washing Machine"* Poet: *Rebecca Kai Dotlich*

Regular Beats/Rhythm	Alliteration
Here's to your spin, your soapsud song (4 beats) your rumble and whirl and twirl along (4 beats)	Here's to your spin, your soapsud song (/s/ sound) your rumble and whirl and twirl along (/r/ sound)
Rhymes	**Repeated Lines**
Here's to your spin, your soapsud song your rumble and whirl and twirl along	Here's to your spin, your soapsud song (first/last lines)

Poetry Lessons to Meet the Common Core State Standards © 2012 by Georgia Heard, Scholastic Teaching Resources

Reading Exemplar Poems in CCSS Appendix B

Many poems in CCSS Appendix B Grades 2–3 Text Exemplars (www.corestandards.org/assets/Appendix_B.pdf) feature multiple musical tools, including the following:

"Who Has Seen the Wind?" by Christina Rossetti

"Knoxville, Tennessee" by Nikki Giovanni

"Eating While Reading" Gary Soto

"Stopping by Woods on a Snowy Evening" by Robert Frost (Text of poem does not appear in CCSS Appendix B.)

Ask students the following questions after reading these poems:

- *Why does the poet repeat the words _____, _____, and _____?*
- *What does this do for the meaning of the poem?*
- *How do repeating the lines _____, _____, and _____ supply rhythm in the poem?*
- *Why does the poet use the words (words that all start with the same letter) _____, _____, and _____?*
- *Which words in the poem rhyme?*
- *Why do you think the poet uses rhyming words?*

CHAPTER 6

Craft and Structure Anchor Standard 4 in Third Grade

CCSS RL 3.4

Determine the meaning of words and phrases as they are used in a text, distinguished from nonliteral language.

I remember cutting a pineapple open once, and my young son exclaimed, "It looks like butterfly wings!" He didn't have to explain the simile to me. Children use figurative language naturally in their everyday talk. The scientist Lewis Thomas wrote: "Children are the best of all at language. We are born . . . with centers of some kind in our brains for . . . manufacturing metaphors. Moreover, we become specialized for this uniquely human function in the early years of our childhood, perhaps losing the mechanism as we mature." Maybe our students should be teaching us about nonliteral language.

Under this standard, first graders learn about sensory and feeling words; in second grade, students are required to describe musical poetic devices; and third graders are introduced to literal and nonliteral language as a prelude to a deeper study of **figurative language** in fifth grade.

In addition, the College and Career Readiness Anchor Standards for Language state that students should demonstrate an understanding of figurative language, word relationships, and nuances in word meanings in kindergarten and grades 1–5.

Although young children speak in metaphor and simile naturally, it's not always as easy for them to understand the metaphors and similes that they encounter in their reading. Yet it is essential for the development of reading comprehension that they have an understanding of literal and nonliteral language. If students haven't had some form of exposure to nonliteral language, they will have difficulty with reading comprehension, not just of poems but in all genres.

Research shows that to convert literal language into a nonliteral meaning, the human mind must conjure memories of the literal image first. In many cases, it's important to create a meaningful scaffold for students to understand figurative language by first building background knowledge through conversation and shared reading. If students have no prior knowledge or memories of the base concrete literal images, it will be difficult for them to imagine a nonliteral meaning. However, we don't want to spend too much time building background knowledge and focusing on the literal images; this will bore young readers because there will be nothing left for them to discover when they finally read the poem.

Demonstration Lesson

Literal and Nonliteral Language

Materials:

✓ Poem: "Dragonfly" by Rebecca Kai Dotlich (p. 73) (display copy and one copy for each student)

✓ Book: informational text about dragonflies, such as *Are You a Dragonfly?* by Judy Allen

✓ Reproducible: Figurative Language Reading Sheet (p. 121) (display copy and one copy for each student)

✓ Chart paper and marker

✓ Colored pencils

Start the exploration in grade 3 with an exploration of what literal and nonliteral language mean. You can share examples of how we use nonliteral language in our everyday lives, such as in the examples below, and brainstorm more with students.

Literal	Nonliteral
It's raining hard.	It's raining cats and dogs.
He ran fast.	He ran like the wind.
Computer that's breaking	Computer virus

Then explain that poets and other writers use nonliteral language because it:

• adds interest.

• awakens the reader's imagination.

• conveys meaning in a more specific way.

• conveys meaning in a more interesting way.

A demonstration lesson might sound like this:

Poets, today I'm going to talk about something all writers do, especially poets. It's one of the truly magical qualities of language. Words can mean one thing on one level and mean something else as well. For example, when we want say that it's raining really hard, we might say, "It's raining cats and dogs."

I'm going to read a poem called "Dragonfly" by Rebecca Kai Dotlich. But before I read the poem, I'd like to ask you to turn and talk to your reading partner about what you already know about dragonflies: how they fly, what they look like, and any facts you know about them. (Give students a chance to share their knowledge of and experience with dragonflies, specifically how dragonflies fly and what they look like. If students have never seen dragonflies and know nothing about them, then show a picture of one, share what you know, and perhaps read an informational book about dragonflies. Then distribute a copy of "Dragonfly" to each student.)

Now, as I read the poem "Dragonfly," listen to how the poet describes this insect.

One strategy that helps readers understand a poem is to draw mind pictures, or imagery, that the words give us. I'd like you to reread the poem independently and draw your mind pictures in the blank space beside the poem. Be sure to use your colored pencils so you can draw the color of the dragonfly.

> ## :: Dragonfly ::
> *by Rebecca Kai Dotlich*
>
> This sky-ballerina,
>
> this glimmering
>
> jewel,
>
> glides in a gown
>
> of lucid blue—
>
> with wings that you
>
> could whisper through.

After students finish drawing, gather them together to share their illustrations and understanding of the poem.

Let's look at how Rebecca Kai Dotlich described a dragonfly. Let's start with the first line: "This sky-ballerina, . . ." I see that some of you drew dragonflies as ballerinas with tutus, and some drew little broken lines to show the way dragonflies fly. What are some of your thoughts about why the poet wrote "sky-ballerina" to describe a dragonfly?

At this point, some students might have taken the poem literally and not understood, for example, that in the first line, the poet is comparing a dragonfly's rather graceful circular flight to a ballerina's dance. As you read through the poem line-by-line, fill out the display copy of the Figurative Language Reading Sheet as shown below. Write down the lines from the poem in the Nonliteral Words column and then illicit from students a literal explanation or interpretation to make the fusion between the two.

Title: *"The Dragonfly"*   Poet: *Rebecca Kai Dotlich*

Nonliteral Words (Figurative language)	Literal Words (Facts)
This sky-ballerina,	Flies in the air loop-de-loop
this glimmering jewel,	different colors like blue and green, shiny
glides in a gown	its wings and body glide
of lucid blue—	clear blue
with wings that you could whisper through.	thin wings, invisible wings

I'm wondering why you think the poet described the dragonfly this way. Why didn't she just state the facts about a dragonfly like we did on the right side of the T-chart?

Give students a chance to talk with their partners and then ask them to share their thinking with the whole class.

When you're reading a poem, a story, or nonfiction, be on the lookout for language that means two things at once: literal and nonliteral. Ask yourself, "Are the words literal (exactly what they mean) or are they nonliteral (have another meaning)? And ask yourself why you think the poet chose to describe the details in the poem this way.

Collaborative Engagement and Independent Application

Use the following activities to extend and assess learning.

Finding Examples in Independent Reading

Have students write in their poetry response journals, on sticky notes, or highlight the nonliteral language they notice in their independent reading.

Creating a T-Chart

Distribute a copy of the Figurative Language Reading Sheet reproducible to each student. Ask students to gather examples of nonliteral language for one side of the chart and then translate it into literal language on the other side of the chart.

Comparing and Contrasting Texts

Challenge students to compare and contrast the poem "Dragonfly" with an informational text on dragonflies, such as *Are You a Dragonfly?* by Judy Allen. Remind them to point out instances of nonliteral language in the informational text.

Reading Exemplar Poems in CCSS Appendix B

Ask students to highlight words, phrases, and lines that use nonliteral language in the following poems in the CCSS Appendix B Grades 2–3 Text Exemplars (www.corestandards. org/assets/Appendix_B.pdf) and to determine their literal meaning:

"Autumn" by Emily Dickinson

"Who Has Seen the Wind?" by Christina Rossetti

"A Bat Is Born" by Randall Jarrell

"Eating While Reading" by Gary Soto

CHAPTER 7

Craft and Structure Anchor Standard 4 in Fifth Grade

CCSS RL 5.4

Determine the meaning of words and phrases as they are used in a text, including figurative language such as metaphors and similes.

I was in the car with my son, who was in fifth grade at the time, and we were stopped at a stoplight. He spotted a Volkswagen Bug with a bumper sticker on it. "Look, Mom," he said, "the person in the car in front of us is probably a little like you—happy."

"How do you know?" I asked.

"Because look at the bumper sticker on her car: 'Wag more. Bark less.'"

"You're right. She probably is happy if she lives by what that bumper sticker says."

"Wag more. Bark less."

Every adult reading that bumper sticker understands what it means.

Think about what we need to do as readers to understand the meaning of this simple bumper sticker wisdom:

We need to know a little something about dogs—that their tails wag when they're happy and that they bark when they're scared or defensive (background knowledge).

We then need to make the cognitive leap that, although the bumper sticker is referring to dogs, it's really advice for humans (figurative language).

My son had just finished a poetry unit of study at his school, and I believe this is what enabled him to understand the bumper sticker's meaning.

Metaphor and Simile

Materials:

- ✓ Poems:

    "A Modern Dragon" by Rowena Bastin Bennett (display copy)—for metaphor

    "Ditchdiggers" excerpt by Lydia Pender (p. 78) (display copy)—for simile

- ✓ Books: informational texts on trains
- ✓ Chart paper and marker
- ✓ Sticky notes
- ✓ Highlighters (in different colors)
- ✓ Reproducible: Visualization Sheet (p. 122)

We've all heard the saying, "A picture is worth a thousand words." One meaning of figurative language is that *figure* means "drawing," "image," or "picture." Figurative language creates figures, or pictures, in the mind of the reader. Authors use concrete literal images as the base from which to make the cognitive leap to compare a startling and seemingly unrelated image to create something new.

The most common figures of speech, or figurative language, are the simile and the metaphor.

- A **simile** is a statement that compares one thing, or image, to another by using the word *like* or *as*.

- A **metaphor** is a statement that compares one thing, or image, to another—without using *like* or *as*. It is an implied comparison.

Metaphor and simile are about learning to describe the world in new ways—in surprising and unique ways. Laurence Perrine wrote, "The mind takes delight in these sudden leaps, in seeing likenesses between unlike things."

WHY POETS AND WRITERS USE METAPHOR AND SIMILE

- To explain and describe something in a unique way
- To help the reader see the unfamiliar in the familiar
- To express emotion
- To make writing more vivid and alive
- To create sight and sound (and other sensory) images

Both metaphor and simile compare two unlike things that have something in common. Robert Bly calls them "forgotten relationships." Bly also says, "The real joy of poetry is to experience this leaping inside a poem."

In the wonderful book *Pyrotechnics on the Page: Playful Craft That Sparks Writing* (2010), Ralph Fletcher writes about metaphor and simile, "They should be front and center in any writer's toolbox because they are fundamental ways to create something new and memorable."

In the spiraling expectations of the CCSS, first-grade students are required to identify words and phrases that suggest feelings or appeal to the senses; third-grade students are introduced to literal and nonliteral language and asked to determine the meaning of that language; and fifth-grade students are required to sharpen their figurative language skills by not only learning about metaphor and simile but also by demonstrating an understanding of the meaning of figurative language.

I initially use poems that have low text complexity to introduce (and review for some students) the concepts of metaphor and simile. Students can then read more complex poems that use metaphor and simile. This is how I introduce a lesson on metaphor and simile to fifth graders:

> *I'm going to show you a drawing. If you look at it one way, you see one thing, and if you look at it another way, you see something completely different.*
>
> *Who sees a vase? Who sees two people staring at each other? Who sees both?*
>
> *Some poems can be a little like this, too. You read them once and you think they're about one thing—their literal meaning, what's happening on the surface—but then you read the poems again, and you realize they're about something totally different. Just like this drawing, sometimes poems have two meanings.*
>
> *I'm going to read to you a poem that is about two things at once, just like this drawing.* (Display "A Modern Dragon" and read it aloud.)
>
> *Who thinks that this poem is about a train? Who thinks this poem is about a dragon? Who thinks it's about both?*
>
> *That's right. It's both—just like the drawing. It's about a train and a dragon at the same time.*

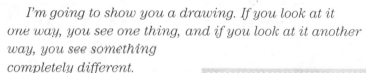

:: A Modern Dragon ::

by Rowena Bastin Bennett

A train is a dragon that roars through the dark.
He wriggles his tail as he sends up a spark.
He pierces the night with his one yellow eye,
And all the earth trembles when he rushes by.

The word for this is metaphor. *A metaphor is when you compare two things that don't seem to be alike, but in comparing them, you find that they are alike. "Modern Dragon" compares a train to a dragon.*

Let's look closely at the poem, at the details, to see how the metaphor of the train and dragon works.

Make a T-chart and read the poem line-by-line. Write down the lines of the poem in the Nonliteral (Metaphor) column and the literal meaning of those lines in the Literal column.

Title: *"Modern Dragon"*   Poet: *Rowena Bastin Bennett*

Nonliteral (Metaphor)	Literal
A train is a dragon that roars through the dark.	Trains roar through the dark because of the sound their engines make. The tails of dragons are long, like trains.
He wriggles his tail as he sends up a spark.	Trains are long like dragons, and when the metal wheels of the train hit the metal tracks, they make sparks.
He pierces the night with his one yellow eye,	Trains have a light at the front to light the way at night.
And all the earth trembles when he rushes by.	Trains are heavy, and when they pass, they make the ground shake.

It's amazing that just like what the drawing shows, words can mean one thing but also mean another.

You can move on to the simile part of the lesson on the same day or introduce it on the next day.

Now I'm going to read part of another poem that compares two things like "Modern Dragon" did, but the comparisons in "Ditchdiggers" are a little different. The poet is comparing machines called ditchdiggers to giraffes, but she uses the word like *in the comparison. Whenever a poet uses the word* like *or as in comparing two things, this is called a simile.*

Let's look at a few lines from "Ditchdiggers." (It might be helpful if you showed students a photograph of a ditchdigger before reading aloud the poem.)

:: Ditchdiggers ::
by Lydia Pender

Like lean giraffes about the building site,
With questing noses tilted to the sky,
They stand, a still and silent little herd. . . .

We'll create a chart to identify the metaphors and similes in this poem. (Set up a chart like the one shown below and then read "Ditchdiggers" aloud again, line by line.)

Title: __"Ditchdiggers"__   Poet: __Lydia Pender__

Actual Lines: Nonliteral	Their Literal Meaning	Type of Figurative Language
Like lean giraffes about the building site,	The digging arm on the machine is long and reaches up into the air.	Simile
With questing noses tilted to the sky,	The end of the digging arm points upward toward the sky and has a cup at the end that holds the dirt.	Metaphor
They stand, a still and silent little herd. . . .	When the ditchdigger machines aren't in use, they are standing together, not making a sound.	Metaphor

In the first line, the poet uses the word like *and compares ditchdiggers to lean giraffes, so we know right away that that's a simile. In the second and third lines, the poet makes a direct comparison, and doesn't use* like *or* as, *so we know they are metaphors: "the questing noses" are the arms of the ditchdigger that reach up toward the sky, and the silent herd (herd means "a group of animals all of the same species") refers to the ditchdiggers standing together when they're not working.*

In all the poems we read today, poets are describing ordinary machines like a train, buses, or ditchdiggers and comparing them to creatures and live animals.

A train becomes a dragon roaring through the dark.

Buses grunt like hippopotamuses.

Ditchdiggers are like lean giraffes.

Why do these poets describe these things this way? Why don't they just say, "A train goes really fast through the dark"; "Bus engines make loud noises"; "I saw a bunch of ditchdiggers all together, and their digging arms are really long and reach up to the sky"?

Give students time to turn and talk with their partners about why the poets used figurative language. On a chart, list the reason why poets use metaphors and similes. Add information from the chart on p. 76 if it's not mentioned by students.

PERSONIFICATION

For an additional lesson on figurative language, explain that "Modern Dragon," "Buses," and "Ditchdiggers" also include examples of **personification**, which is when the poet gives inanimate objects human qualities.

Collaborative Engagement and Independent Application

Use the following activities to extend and assess the learning.

Acting Out a Poem

Have students act out "Modern Dragon" by Rowena Bastin Bennett or another poem such as "Fog" by Carl Sandburg in CCSS Appendix B. Direct students to read the poem line-by-line and figure out how best to act it out. They can discuss whether they will be acting out a literal train or a nonliteral dragon.

Naming the Details

Ask students to identify and write down the details in "Modern Dragon" that describe both the train and the dragon or other poems that contain metaphor and simile.

Illustrating a Poem

Encourage students to illustrate "Modern Dragon" or other poems that contain metaphor and simile by paying particular attention to the words the poet uses to describe the metaphors and similes. They can use the Visualization Sheet for their illustrations and then write what they think the poet's message is.

Comparing and Contrasting Texts

Set out informational texts on trains and have students compare and contrast "Modern Dragon" with one of them. How do the two approaches on the same topic compare?

Identifying Similes and Metaphors in Other Poems

As students read poems, stories, and other texts, they can identify and collect examples of similes and metaphors in their poetry response journals or on sticky notes to share with the class. Ask students to identify and highlight metaphors in one color and similes in another color, then write *s* for simile and *m* for metaphor next to the examples.

Reading Exemplar Poems in CCSS Appendix B

Many poems in CCSS Appendix B Grades 4–5 Text Exemplars (www.corestandards.org/assets/Appendix_B.pdf) use figurative language. Ask students to highlight similes and metaphors in the following poems and discuss how figurative language helps convey meaning in each one:

"The Echoing Green" by William Blake

"The New Colossus" by Emma Lazarus

"A Bird Came Down the Walk" by Emily Dickinson

"Fog" by Carl Sandburg

"Words Free as Confetti" by Pat Mora

Introduction to Craft and Structure Anchor Standard 5

CCSS Craft & Structure 5

Analyze the structure of texts, including how specific sentences, paragraphs, and larger portions of text (e.g., a section, chapter, scene, or stanza) relate to each other and the whole.

A poem is like a house. Metaphorically, it has to have a foundation, walls, and a roof for it to work. The basic building block of **prose** is the sentence, but in poetry, it's the line. If you write or type a story, it doesn't matter where the lines end, but in poetry, where the lines end is crucial to the structure of the poem.

This anchor standard expects students to understand and be able to explain the inherent structure of three main literary genres: poetry, story, and drama. The chart on page 83 shows what this continuum looks like, as it concerns poetry, in kindergarten and grades 3–5. Note that the focus is on story in grades 1 and 2, so they are not included in the chart or in this section.

The Structure of Poetry

Since a poem's underlying structure is the line, each line of a poem is a unit of meaning, and lines are grouped together with other lines into stanzas.

Stanza comes from the Italian word meaning "room." A poem might have one or several stanzas, just as a house or an apartment might have different rooms: a kitchen for cooking and eating, a bedroom for sleeping, a family room for relaxing, and so on. When we encounter a poem, we see its visual aspects first. We notice instantly if the poem has stanzas or if the lines are written all together in one block with no break. We also glance at the length of the lines and the length of the poem.

Craft and Structure Anchor Standard 5 Continuum

Kindergarten	Grade 3	Grade 4	Grade 5
Recognize common types of texts (e.g., storybooks, **poems**)	Refer to parts of stories, dramas, and **poems** when writing or speaking about a text, using terms such as chapter, scene, and **stanza**; describe how each successive part builds on earlier sections.	Explain major differences between **poems**, drama, and prose, and **refer to the structural elements of poems (e.g., verse, rhythm, meter)** and drama (e.g., casts of characters, settings, descriptions, dialogue, stage directions) when writing or speaking about a text.	Explain how a series of chapters, scenes, or **stanzas** fits together to provide the overall structure of a particular story, drama, or **poem**.

As we read and reread, we become aware that the structure of a poem not only supports its meaning but also helps convey it. In high school and college, we frequently analyze the structural elements of a poem, its meter and rhyme, as a way to understand its meaning. But isn't that putting the cart before the horse? Before readers are motivated to analyze the structure of a poem, they must be able to connect to the experience of the poem to understand its meaning.

Understanding the structure of a poem and being able to articulate that understanding requires students to have a more rigorous knowledge of poetry as they progress through the grades.

When we speak about a poem's structure we mean the following:

- line
- stanza
- rhythm
- meter
- form

Students should know that most poetry falls into two categories:

- free verse
- formal poetry

Free verse is not, as many people think, structureless: it has lines and stanzas, rhythm, and may use other poetic devices like repetition or rhyme. Free verse uses the cadences or natural rhythms of speech. It does not conform to a predetermined form or pattern, but it still has structure. Free verse is an organic form—meaning that the structure emerges from the thought or feeling being expressed.

Formal poetry has a predetermined, uniform, and regular pattern of lines, rhythm, and stanzas. The **sonnet**, for example, is either 14 or 16 lines long (depending on what kind of sonnet it is) and written in iambic pentameter. There are modern variations on the sonnet, but it has been written using the same form for centuries.

The CCSS expects students to read and understand the structure of both free verse and formal poetry. The following chapters focus on teaching poetic structure in kindergarten and grades 3–5.

CHAPTER 8

Craft and Structure Anchor Standard 5 in Kindergarten

CCSS RL K.5

Recognize common types of texts (e.g., storybooks, poems).

In a kindergarten class, I introduced myself as a poet and asked if anyone knew what a poet was. One boy raised his hand and said, "Something that swims in water." I smiled and thought to myself that it was as good a definition as any.

The best way to understand the meaning of poetry is to hear and read a lot of it. Kindergarten students should be exposed to a wide variety of print, including poetry. During read-aloud, we can ask children to help us identify the different types of texts, their characteristics, and language conventions—and ask the question, "What makes a poem different from a story?" Although this standard is for kindergarten students, knowledge of the characteristics of different texts and genre types should be revisited in every grade.

Children will develop their understanding of what poetry is as you read poems aloud to them, as they see poems in books and displayed on classroom walls, and as you have conversations with them about the characteristics of poetry. You can generate and display a What We Know About Poetry chart as an ongoing reference that you revisit throughout the year.

Demonstration Lesson

Poems Look Different From Stories

Materials:

✓ Poem: "Oak Tree" by Georgia Heard (p. 86)
✓ Books:
  Falling Down the Page: A Book of List Poems by Georgia Heard

A Meal of the Stars: Poems Up and Down by Dana Jensen

a variety of poetry books and story books

✓ Chart paper and marker

✓ Sticky notes

✓ Baskets or bins

The most obvious difference between a story and a poem is the way a poem looks on the page. Young readers can simply glance at a poem without even reading it and be able to recognize poetry because it looks different from stories.

I begin by describing a poem's shape as being like a tall building—longer and thinner than most stories. Then I display a poem with short lines to show children the shape of a poem and to compare it to the words in a storybook. I also point out that the lines in a poem are usually shorter than a story.

For this lesson, choose poems that have an obvious shape: poems with short lines; poems with several stanzas; long, thin poems that resemble tall buildings. (This doesn't mean a **concrete poem**, which is a poem whose shape is composed to match its theme; for example, a poem about ice cream in the shape of an ice cream cone.) If you introduce concrete poems too early, children will think that all poems are written in the shape of their topic.

"Booktime" and "Oak Tree" have an obvious " poem shape." (Read "Oak Tree" from bottom to top.)

Write a couple of long, thin poems on chart paper to display. Also, choose one or more picture books to show children. Then begin the lesson.

You've listened to stories and poems read aloud since the first day of school. Today, I want to show you something about poetry that you might have noticed before. Did you ever notice

Sky

Touching

Up

Up

Up

Reaching

Up

Up

Up

Climbs

Acorn

Small

One

:: **Oak Tree** ::

by Georgia Heard

HOW TO RECOGNIZE A POEM

- Poems look different from stories. Sometimes they look like tall buildings or small boxes.
- Poems are shorter than stories.
- Poems have shorter lines.
- Poems have white space around the words.

that poems look different from stories? One way to tell the difference between a poem and a story is that poems look different from stories. Most of the time you can look at a poem and, without even reading it, you can see that it's a poem.

Look at these poems, and look at this story. See how these poems are long and skinny and look like tall buildings? Stories are written all the way across the page like this one.

I'm going to take this marker and draw a line around the outside of each poem so we can see its shape even better.

Poems have shorter lines, and sometimes they even have only one word on a line.

Now, not every poem is this long and thin. Some look more like boxes. We'll be reading and seeing a lot of poems. When you see a poem, remember that it is different from a story.

Collaborative Engagement and Independent Application

Use the following activities to extend and assess learning.

Drawing a Poem's Shape

Have small groups or the entire class use markers to draw an outline around the outside of poems to show the shapes. Ask: *What kinds of shapes do you see? How are the shapes of poems different from the shapes of stories?*

Categorizing Poetry Books and Storybooks

In this activity, students may work independently or in pairs or small groups. Allow students to browse through poetry books and storybooks. Once they determine a book's genre, have them write a *P* for Poetry and an *S* for Story on a sticky note and attach it to the book. Make labels for poetry bins or baskets and ask students to place the poetry books in the basket. Have a conversation about how children determined whether a book is a poetry book or a storybook.

Demonstration Lesson

Recognizing Poetry

Materials:

✓ Poems:
   "Saturday" by Kay Winters (p. 88) (display copy)
   A variety of nursery rhymes and rhyming poems

✓ Books:
   Over in the Pink House by Rebecca Kai Dotlich
   Saturdays and Teacakes by Lester Laminack
   A variety of picture books, informational texts, and poetry collections

✓ Markers
✓ What We Know About Poetry chart (see p. 85)

Poems are visually different from stories, but they also have other inherent qualities that make them poems. Begin introducing poetry to kindergarten children by reading nursery rhymes and other poems that rhyme, rhythmic poems, or repetitive poems, because these are more easily recognizable as poems, and then discuss characteristics of poems. You can also read jump rope rhymes from *Over in the Pink House*.

After children are familiar with this more singsong kind of poetry, it's essential to read a wide range of poetry that uses different poetic tools: poems that give children pictures in their minds; poems that use figurative language; and nonrhyming poetry. Too many primary teachers read only rhyming poetry to young children and miss the wonderful variety of poetry. This is how I might teach this lesson:

> We've been talking about what poetry is, and how a poem is different from a story. We already know that a poem has a different shape than a story.
>
> But there are other qualities that make up a poem. We're going to be reading a lot of poems throughout the year and adding to our *What We Know About Poetry* chart. (Display a copy of "Saturday.") I'm going to read you this poem called "Saturday," and afterward we can talk about what you notice about it. As I read, let's clap our hands to the rhythm of the poem.

After reading the poem, ask children what they notice. Here are some of the qualities they will identify and that you can write on the What We Know About Poetry chart:

- Looks different from a story
- Has a rhythm or a beat
- Has a few short words on a line
- Rhymes
- Is short
- Repeats words
- Is rhythmic like a song

As you continue to read poems aloud to students, they will notice other qualities, such as the following, that you can add to the chart:

- Tells feelings
- Makes you laugh
- Gives you a picture in your mind

:: Saturday ::

by Kay Winters

It's my day.
A "hi" day.

A run day.
A fun day.

A me day.
A see day.

A who day?
A you day?

A can't-wait-to-play day.
I hope-you-can-stay day.

Collaborative Engagement and Independent Application

Use the following activities to extend and assess learning.

Acting Out a Poem

Working with the entire class or small groups, have students act out "Saturday." Scaffold the poem by reading it line-by-line and rehearsing possible actions and gestures with students. For example, for the lines "It's my day/A 'hi' day," students might point to themselves and wave, as if saying "hi."

Highlighting Craft

With your support, ask students to listen for and help you highlight the repeating word "day" at the end of every line in "Saturday" and discuss why the poet repeated this word. If you haven't already done so, add rhyme and repetition to the What We Know About Poetry chart

Drawing a Poem's Shape

Give copies of several poems to students. Then tell them to draw an outline around each poem with a marker and discuss how the shape of a poem is different from that of a story.

Shared Writing

Encourage students to share the fun things they do on Saturdays. Work with the class to create a shared list poem about their experiences.

Illustrating a Poem

Students can illustrate one fun thing they do on Saturdays and share it with the class. Compare their experiences with the descriptions of the day in "Saturday."

Comparing and Contrasting Texts

Read aloud and compare the poem "Saturday" with the picture book *Saturdays and Teacakes* by Lester Laminack. Discuss with students the differences and similarities between these two types of texts on the same subject.

Identifying Poetry

Even if students aren't yet reading, they will come to identify the different genres by their features, such as the "look" of a poem or photos and graphics in a nonfiction text. Show students a poem, a picture book, and an informational text and ask them to identify the genre of each text. Ask questions like the following:

- *What kind of text are you reading?*
- *How do you know that this is a poem?*
- *Do you remember some of the characteristics of poetry on our What We Know About Poetry chart?*
- *Do you see any of those characteristics in the poem you're reading or that I read aloud to you?*

Finding Similarities Between Poems and Stories

Many stories share some of the same craft tools as poems: repetition, rhyme, imagery, and so on. After students have listened to poems for a while and their understanding of poetry has grown, you can explore how stories can also share some of the same qualities as poems—particularly those in picture books.

With students' input, create a Venn diagram highlighting the differences and similarities between stories and poems.

Read Exemplar Poems in CCSS Appendix B

Read aloud and discuss some of the free verse and traditional exemplar poems in Appendix B of the CCSS for K–1 (www.corestandards.org/assets/Appendix_B.pdf) and add students' observations to the What We Know About Poetry chart.

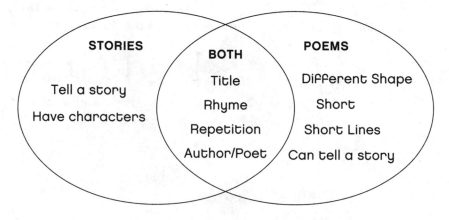

STORIES

Tell a story

Have characters

BOTH

Title

Rhyme

Repetition

Author/Poet

POEMS

Different Shape

Short

Short Lines

Can tell a story

Craft and Structure Anchor Standard 5 in Third Grade

CCSS RL 3.5

Refer to parts of stories, dramas, and poems when writing or speaking about a text, using terms such as chapter, scene, and stanza; describe how each successive part builds on earlier sections.

When my son was six and we would go out to dinner, he would make buildings and structures out of anything he could find. He took sugar packets out of their holder to build buildings, added a few toothpicks and salt and pepper shakers for support, a knife for a ramp, and by the end of the meal he would have built a city. The server usually looked worriedly at the sugar packets piled high on the table, but we were always careful to clean up before we left.

All texts—including stories, poems, and drama—have a structure, a means of organizing words, thoughts, ideas, and experiences. In stories, writers use the sentence and the paragraph to organize. In poetry, poets use lines and stanzas.

This standard expects third-grade students not only to identify what a stanza is but also to understand how stanzas help organize the ideas, images, and meaning of a poem as it progresses from beginning to end.

Demonstration Lesson

Stanzas

Materials:

✓ Poems:
  "Sand House" by J. Patrick Lewis (p. 92) (display copy and copy to cut up)
  Poems with two-, three-, and four-line stanzas
✓ A variety of chapter books, dramas, and poems to compare

✓ Scissors

✓ Drawing paper and art materials, such as colored pencils and markers

I like to use "Sand House" by J. Patrick Lewis to introduce this lesson.

Poets, today I'm going to read a poem called "Sand House" by J. Patrick Lewis. But before I read the poem aloud, I want you to take a look at how it looks on the page. What do you notice about it?

That's right, the poem looks like it has paragraphs like a story does. But in poetry, these blocks of words are not called paragraphs; they're called stanzas.

The word stanza *means "room" in Italian. So, without even reading the poem, just by looking at it, you can see that it has four "rooms": maybe a living room, kitchen, bedroom, and dining room. Also, notice that each stanza has four lines in it. Poets like to use stanzas to organize their poems visually as well as to organize their ideas, thoughts, and feelings.*

As I read this poem aloud, keep in mind that it is divided into four stanzas, or rooms.

(Read aloud "Sand House," pausing between each stanza.)

Now, if this were a house, and we could walk through each room, what would you see in each room? Let's look at the first stanza. What's happening here?

In this first stanza, the speaker says he built a sand house in the afternoon with a bucket, cup, and tablespoon.

In the second stanza, the speaker says he scooped with a shovel more sand and made a second floor of the sand house.

In the third stanza, the speaker says, "But when the fingers/Of the sea/Reached up and waved/A wave to me." What do you think this means? (The poem's figurative language describing the sea will probably be clear to many third graders, but it's important to clarify the use of metaphor in this stanza.) *A wave comes up to the sand house . . . and what happened?*

In the fourth stanza, the sand house tumbles down and disappears between the speaker's toes. (You might have to explain the expression "tumbled down/Like dominoes" as it is used in this context.)

I'd like us to think about the way J. Patrick Lewis uses stanzas in "Sand House." What do you think the poem would be like if it didn't have any stanzas at all? If it

> ## :: Sand House ::
> *by J. Patrick Lewis*
>
> I built a house
> One afternoon
> With bucket, cup
> And tablespoon.
>
> Then scooped a shovel
> Full of shore
> On top to add
> The second floor.
>
> But when the fingers
> Of the sea
> Reached up and waved
> A wave to me,
>
> It tumbled down
> Like dominoes
> And disappeared
> Between my toes.

were just one block of words? (You can write a poem as a block of words without stanzas to show students the difference.)

Turn to your reading partner and explain why you think this poet used stanzas in the poem.

Here are some of the explanations my students have come up with:

- "It separates the words into packages of ideas."

- "It kind of slows the action down."

- "It makes us pay attention to the poem. It would be too fast without them."

- "It's like each stanza is a little piece of the story."

The poem tells a story of the speaker building a sand house at the beach, adding more sand for a second floor, and then a wave comes, and the sand house tumbles down and disappears between his toes.

STANZAS

It's helpful for students to first understand some of the reasons poets use stanzas.

- Organize ideas by isolating separate events, images, or thoughts.
- Give readers time to pause and think.
- Divide a narrative into actions.
- Slow down the reading of a poem.
- Provide a visual structure.
- Draw the reader's attention to one thought or one image.
- Create suspense, tension, or interest when readers continue to the next stanza.
- Keep two or more speakers separate.

Collaborative Engagement and Independent Application

Use the following activities to extend and assess learning.

Having a Conversation to Grow Ideas

Give students the opportunity to read several other poems that have stanzas with partners. Find poems that have two-, three-, and four-line stanzas and ask students to talk about why they think the poet chose to use that kind of stanza, and how the stanzas support the meaning of the poem. Pose a prompt such as the following: *Explain how the last stanza brings the ideas presented in the poem together. Be sure to use examples from the poem in your explanation.*

Reordering Stanzas

Cut up the stanzas in "Sand House," rearrange them, and then ask students to try putting the stanzas in order according to the sequence of the action. Afterward, have a conversation about how students knew how to put the stanzas in the order they did. Was the order of the stanzas clear from the images, actions, or transition words like *then* and *but*?

Acting Out a Poem

Ask the entire class or a small group to act out "Sand House" or another poem, stanza by stanza. Ask students to consider whether each stanza has a separate image or action that they can act out.

Illustrating Stanzas

Students can illustrate a poem, stanza by stanza, to help clarify the progression from one stanza to the next. Ask them to think about the following questions:

- *Does each stanza convey a separate image or does the stanza contain a continuation of an image begun in a previous stanza?*
- *What is the progression of images in each stanza?*

They can use separate sheets of paper to illustrate each stanza and then compile them in a small booklet.

Comparing and Contrasting Texts

Read a chapter book, short drama, and poem, and compare and contrast the differences and similarities between the poem's stanzas, the chapter book's chapters, and the drama's scenes.

Reading Exemplar Poems in CCSS Appendix B

Ask students to read and respond to the poems below in Appendix B of the CCSS for 2–3 (www.corestandards.org/assets/Appendix_B.pdf). Have them refer to stanzas when writing or speaking about the poems, paying particular attention to how the stanzas progress and build on one another to convey meaning.

"Autumn" by Emily Dickinson

"Who Has Seen the Wind?" by Christina Rossetti

"Afternoon on a Hill" by Edna St. Vincent Millay

"Stopping by Woods on a Snowy Evening" by Robert Frost*

"Eating While Reading" by Gary Soto

"Something Told the Wild Geese" by Rachel Field*

"Weather" by Eve Merriam*

* Text of poem does not appear in CCSS Appendix B.

CHAPTER 10

Craft and Structure Anchor Standard 5 in Fourth Grade

CCSS RL 4.5

Explain major differences between poems, drama, and prose, and refer to structural elements of poems (e.g., verse, rhythm, meter) and drama (e.g., casts of characters, settings, descriptions, dialogue, stage directions) when writing or speaking about a text.

The two questions that I'm asked most when I give poetry workshops are, "What is poetry?" and "What's the difference between prose and poetry?"

People have been trying to define what poetry is for centuries. I think the best explanations are by poets themselves:

- "Poetry is the spontaneous overflow of powerful feelings." —*William Wordsworth*

- "Poetry is the journal of a sea animal living on land, wanting to fly in the air." —*Carl Sandburg*

- "Poetry is what in a poem makes you laugh, cry, prickle, be silent, makes your toenails twinkle . . ." —*Dylan Thomas*

These explanations define poetry's emotional effects. A more prosaic definition of poetry—and the only real difference between poetry and prose—involves its structure. Prose is organized around sentences and paragraphs, and poetry is defined by its lines and stanzas.

The majority of the reading students do in school is prose. Yet if you ask most students to define prose, they would have a difficult time doing so. The dictionary definition of prose is that it's the most typical form of language that applies ordinary grammatical structure and the natural flow of speech such as in novels, newspapers, magazines, and so on. Most students know a couple of prose elements, such as that paragraphs are organized around a clear main idea and that details support the main idea. But defining the characteristics of poetry is not given the same amount of attention in most elementary classrooms. Students read or listen to

poems occasionally but don't usually spend days and weeks studying a particular poem and learning poetry's characteristics.

For this standard, students in grade 4 are expected to understand the major differences inherent in the structures of poetry, story, and drama, and to be able to explain those major differences in writing or speaking. For poetry, the main structural elements are verse, rhythm, and meter.

Demonstration Lesson

Verse

Materials:

✓ A variety of poems

✓ Chart paper and marker

✓ Sheets of paper

The word *verse* has several meanings. Verse is synonymous with poetry, referring specifically to poetry that has a metrical or rhythmic structure. **Blank verse** is a type of poetry having regular meter but no rhyme. And free verse is poetry written without the use of strict meter or rhyme, because it uses the cadence or natural rhythms of speech.

Verse also means a single line of poetry, which is what this standard is referring to in the list of poetic structural elements (e.g., verse, rhythm, meter). **Verse**, or **line**, is the main organizational unit of a poem.

When prose is written on a page, it doesn't matter where the lines end, but in poetry the words are arranged deliberately in lines. In poetry, as in music, there is a tension between sound and silence. It's both the words on the page as well as the white space or silence on the page that work to create this music. Michael Harper (2009) writes: "The most important thing in a poem is silence. Yes, you know, all voids are not to be filled . . . some space has to be left there to resonate. It is often the absence of sound, what it not going on."

It is the line or verse, and where that line ends, also called the **line break**, that builds the structure of a poem and also gives a poem its music, rhythm, and form. In formal poetry with a set meter, rhythm, or form, the lines are predetermined by the form or the meter. In other words, in a sonnet all lines will be iambic pentameter or ten syllables long (i.e., five iambic feet; see explanation of meter on pp. 98–101.) Whereas in a free verse poem, lines are written in the following ways:

- to coincide with the natural breath or pause
- to emphasize a particular word or words
- to change the pace of the poem
- to enhance the visual impact of the poem
- to organize a poem, lines can either be **end-stopped**, meaning that a thought, action, or image ends at the end of the line; or **run-on**, where the thought, action, or image continues onto the next line (a technique also called **enjambment**: the break at the end of the line interrupts the natural rhythm or grammar and is dragged onto the next line). Poets enjamb their poems for many reasons:

- to create tension
- to disguise rhyme
- to vary the rhythm and pace of a poem

To begin this lesson on verse, I remind students what we know about stanzas:

We've talked about how a poem is a little bit like a house in that it sometimes has different stanzas, or rooms, in it, but let's look even more closely at the poem/house. The stanzas, or rooms, are made up of lines. When you read a story, it really doesn't matter where the lines end on a page. But in poetry, the poet has a purpose when he or she places the words on a line. So let's say we want to copy a poem from a book. We would have to write every line exactly as it is written, including exactly where the line begins and ends.

I'm going to divide a sentence—that is, not a line from poetry—into three different line variations. I'll read the sentences aloud, and I'd like you to notice how the meaning and the rhythm of the sentence change depending on where the lines are broken and where my voice pauses. (Write the sentences below on chart paper so students can see the visual difference between the three variations.)

1. *Snow falls lightly over the grass.* (Read the sentence all the way through like you would prose.)
2. *Snow falls* (pause)
   lightly (pause)
   over the grass.
3. *Snow* (pause)
   falls (pause)
   lightly (pause)
   over (pause)
   the grass. (pause)

I'd like you to tell your reading partner what you think the difference is between the first, second, and third ways I read the sentence.

Some of my students' responses are shown below:

"The second and third way you read is slower."

"The third way is really slow."

"In the second and third reading, the words have rhythm."

"In the third reading, it gives us time to think."

"The way the third one is written is like snow falling down."

You noticed that when I change where the lines end, it changes the rhythm and even the meaning of the sentence. This is exactly how the lines in a poem work, too. Whenever you see white space after a line, or between stanzas, it means silence—and the reader should pause. The lines of a poem are written to show us how the poet wants the poem read, knowing that any time a reader sees white space it means to pause.

So, no matter what kind of poem it is—rhymed, rhythmic, or in a set form—we need to pay attention to the verses or lines when we read it.

Collaborative Engagement and Independent Application

Use the following activities to extend and assess learning.

Working With Lines and Line Breaks

Write several types of poems (free verse, rhymed, and formal, such as a limerick) on separate sheets of paper as paragraphs by taking out the line breaks. Challenge partners to determine where they think the lines of each poem should end and mark them with a slash mark. Students can then read the original poems and discuss their decisions and why they think the poets broke the lines where they did.

Discussing Lines and Line Breaks

Guide students in finding a poem that they like and have them discuss with partners how the lines and line breaks in the poem support its meaning.

(See additional activities at end of this chapter on pp. 00–00.)

Demonstration Lesson

Rhythm and Meter

Materials:

- ✓ Poems:
  "Birches" excerpt by Robert Frost (p. 100) (display copy and one copy for each student)
  "Casey at the Bat" by Ernest Lawrence Thayer (www.corestandards.org/assets/Appendix_B.pdf) (one copy for each student)
- ✓ Chart paper and marker

When I taught poetry to graduate students at Teachers College, Columbia University, and it came time to discuss meter, my students rolled their eyes and groaned. I would then ask everyone to place their hands on their hearts, listen to the rhythm, and write that rhythm down on paper in whatever form they wanted, for example:

duh/DUH duh/DUH

Ba/BUMP Ba/BUMP

Then I would read a love poem by Shakespeare and ask them to listen to the rhythm of the words: "Thou ART/more LOVE/ly AND/more TEM/per ATE . . .

"Isn't the rhythm of this Shakespeare line similar to the rhythm of your heart?" I'd ask.

The Greeks called this rhythm, or meter, *iambic*. One iamb consists of an unstressed syllable and a stressed syllable, which is written as u/. This is just one example of **meter**. To make it more complicated, five iambs on one line is called **iambic pentameter**: u/u/u/u/u/ (*penta* means "five"). When people study these various kinds of meter in poetry, this is called **prosody**. And when a reader reads a poem to find its meter, this is called **scanning** a poem.

Iambic is the most common and natural form of rhythm because it sounds like the rhythm of our hearts (u/u/u/u/u/). There are other kinds of meter as well.

Kinds of Meter	
Trochee: DA/dum	/u
Spondee: DA/DA	//
Anapest: da da/DUM	uu/
Dactyl: DA/dum/dum	/uu

The discussion about meter and rhythm doesn't have to be boring and academic. **Rhythm** is one of the key ingredients of poetry. The regular repetition of a beat (which students were required to learn about in second grade); the rise and fall of syllables (stressed and unstressed); and the arrangement of them from word to word and line to line is what gives poetry its music.

Rita Dove said, "This is my absolute bias: If a poem doesn't sing, I have no use for it. I simply haven't. Of course there are many kinds of songs. Let's put it this way: If the very sound of those words, the patterns heard in the way they're put down and work together—if that doesn't affect you on some level that cannot be explained in words, then the poem hasn't done its job. It has to keep singing all the way, or at least end in song" (Alexander, 2005).

I begin this lesson on rhythm and meter for fourth graders the same way I began it for my graduate students:

I'd like you to place your hands on your hearts. Do you feel its rhythm? Your heart has a regular beat. How would you describe it: Da/DUM Da/DUM or Ba/BUMP Ba/BUMP?

Well, I want to tell you something about poetry. Just like your heart has a beat, many poems also have a regular beat that gives them their rhythm. Some poems even have the exact same rhythm as your heart. In poetry, when a poem has a regular beat like this, we call it the poem's meter or rhythm.

So let me try to write a line about the weather today in the same meter and rhythm as our hearts. (Write the lines on chart paper; capitalize the stressed syllables.) *It might go something like this:*

ToDAY is CLOUdy, RAINy and COLD.

Do you hear the rhythm: da/DUM da/DUM da/DUM da/DUM? One syllable is weak or softer (unstressed), and the next syllable is strong or louder (stressed).

Or I could write about something you might have said this morning:

I SAID good MORNing TO my MOM.

Do you hear the same rhythm: da/DUM da/DUM da/DUM da/DUM?

If we were writing a poem, this would be the poem's rhythm or meter, and it would be the same in every line. This kind of meter, da/DUM, is called an iamb. *One of those da/DUMs is called something really funny: an iambic foot. A* **foot** *means "one unit of meter." If you have five of these feet (da/DUM da/DUM da/DUM da/DUM da/DUM), that's called* iambic pentameter—penta *means "five." This is the most typical meter used in English poetry.*

Let's read a few lines and listen for the meter. (Distribute a copy of "Birches" to each student.)

Take your pencils, and as I read the poem aloud, I'd like you to mark the rhythm that

you hear. Make a small u for the weak or softer syllable and a slant line for the strong or louder syllable. These are the first two lines of Robert Frost's wonderful poem "Birches":

When I/see BIR/ches BEND/to LEFT/and RIGHT
aCROSS/the LINES/of STRAIGHT/ter DAR/ker TREES,

What does the meter look like? We would write it as u/u/u/u/u/.
Let's count. How many feet are in this line? Yes, there are five feet.
Did anyone recognize the meter? That's right, it's iambic pentameter.
Many poems written before the last 50 years have a regular rhythm and meter, and they often rhyme as well.
I'm going to give you a few lines from several poems, and I would like you to read them with your reading partners, paying particular attention to the rhythm or the meter of each poem. Can you tell whether the poem has a set meter or rhyme? Can you scan and mark the poem's meter? Remember, that's when you listen for the poem's rhythm or meter and mark it with a stress mark for the weak or soft syllable and an unstressed mark for the stronger or louder syllable.

Write the following lines of poetry on a sheet of paper and make a copy for each student (stressed syllables appear in boldface and the meter is in parentheses, for your reference only):

Tyger, **Ty**ger, **bur**ning **bright**	(/u/u/u/)
In the **for**ests **of** the **night**	(/u/u/u/)
—from "Tyger, Tyger Burning Bright" by William Blake	
Shall **I** com**pare** thee **to** a **sum**mer's **day**?	(u/u/u/u/u/)
—from "Sonnet 18" by William Shakespeare	
The **sun** does **rise**	(u/u/)
and **make hap**py the **skies**	(u//uu/)
—from "The Echoing Green" by William Blake	
(The full text appears in CCSS Appendix B Grades 4–5)	
Something **told** the **wild geese**	(/u/u//)
It was **time** to **go**.	(/u/u/)
—from "Something Told the Wild Geese" by Rachel Field	
(The full text appears in CCSS Appendix B Grade band 4–5)	

As students are reading and listening to a poem's rhythm and meter, remind them that people might hear the same poem's meter in slightly different ways. For example, Shakespeare's line, "**Shall I** com**pare** thee **to** a **sum**mer's **day**?" might also be heard as

(//u/u/u/u/), with two stressed syllables in the first two words of the line. Nobody knows which way Shakespeare heard the rhythm as he wrote the line. Emphasize that it's not important to hear every syllable exactly like everyone else hears it.

Collaborative Engagement and Independent Application

Use the following activities to extend and assess learning.

Reading a Poem With Your Ears

Ask students to choose a favorite poem to read aloud. Then say the following: *Your ears will notice what your eyes might miss. Listen to the rhythm of the poem—does it have a regular beat? Does it have a set meter? Reread the poem and mark the beats to see if it has a set meter, and read the poem aloud, reflecting the rhythm you've identified.*

Noticing the Visual Structure of a Poem

Select a poem for students to read or have them choose their own. Tell students to notice the way the poem looks on the page. Remind them that the visual organization or form of the poem may reveal something about its meter. Ask students to discuss what they notice with their partner. Then read the poem and scan its meter to check their observations.

Noticing the Structural Elements of a Poem

Ask students to do the following performance task from CCSS Appendix B:

> *Have students analyze Ernest Lawrence Thayer's "Casey at the Bat" and identify the structural elements (e.g., verse, rhythm, meter), contrasting the impact and differences of those elements to a prose summary of the poem.*

Writing Poetry: Free Verse and Meter/Rhythm/Rhyme

Tell students to do the following:

- Choose a poem that's written in meter, rhythm, and rhyme. Rewrite the poem as a free verse poem. How does that change the poem?

- Choose a poem that's written in free verse. Then try rewriting the poem with rhyme, rhythm, and meter. How does that change the poem?

Responding to Questions

Write the following questions on the board or chart paper:

- *How do the structural elements of this poem help the poet convey meaning? Use examples from the poem in your analysis.*

- *What are the structural elements of a poem? How do they contribute to a poem? How do they help the reader understand the poem or its message?*

Then let students select a poem and respond to the questions in their poetry response journals after reading it.

Reading Exemplar Poems in CCSS Appendix B: Scanning Meter

Ask students to read these poems that use meter from CCSS Appendix B, grades 4–5 (www. corestandards.org/assets/Appendix_B.pdf). Tell them to scan the meter of each poem, marking each line with stress and unstressed marks. Finally, direct them to discuss with a partner how the meter informs the poem's meaning.

"The Echoing Green" by William Blake

"The New Colossus" by Emma Lazarus

"Casey at the Bat" by Ernest Lawrence Thayer

"A Bird Came Down the Walk" by Emily Dickinson

"Dust of Snow" by Robert Frost*

"Little Red Riding Hood and the Wolf" by Roald Dahl*

"They Were My People" by Grace Nichols*

Reading Exemplar Poems in CCSS Appendix B: Verse, Rhythm, or Meter

Direct students to read aloud the poems below from CCSS Appendix B:

"The Echoing Green" by William Blake

"Casey at the Bat" by Ernest Lawrence Thayer

"A Bird Came Down the Walk" by Emily Dickinson

"Fog" by Carl Sandburg

"Dust of Snow" by Robert Frost*

"Little Red Riding Hood and the Wolf" by Roald Dahl*

"They Were My People" by Grace Nichols*

Have them discuss the meaning and identify the structural elements of each poem. Ask students to answer questions like the following:

- *Which poems are written in free verse?*
- *Which poems have a set meter and form?*
- *What meter do the poems use, and is the meter regular or does it change?*
- *What do you notice about the lines and line breaks in each poem?*

* Text of poem does not appear in CCSS Appendix B.

CHAPTER 11

Craft and Structure Anchor Standard 5 in Fifth Grade

CCSS RL 5.5

Explain how a series of chapters, scenes, or stanzas fits together to provide the overall structure of a particular story, drama, or poem.

In a fifth-grade class, a student wrote a free verse poem about friendship. Because of the subject matter of his poem, he decided to write it in two-line stanzas, or couplets. When I conferred with the student, he explained that he arranged his stanzas in couplets because the poem was about friendship, and that it takes two people to be friends—thus, the two-line stanzas. Here's a student who understood that poetic structure and meaning are entwined.

This fifth-grade standard returns to the poetic device of the stanza. In third grade, students are expected to use terms such as *stanza* appropriately in referring to poems and describing how the successive parts of a poem build upon earlier sections. In other words, third-grade students are expected to be able to identify what a stanza is and to understand the relationship between stanzas and the development from one stanza to the next.

Now, in fifth grade, students are expected to be knowledgeable about how stanzas work and to also understand how stanzas affect the overall structure and meaning of a poem.

Demonstration Lesson

How Stanzas Provide Structure

Materials:

✓ Poem: "My People" by Langston Hughes (p. 104) (display copy and a copy to cut up)

✓ Three sheets of drawing paper for each student

✓ Colored pencils or markers

✓ Scissors

Fifth-grade students must have knowledge of the different types of stanzas. Below are descriptions of the most common types:

- A two-line stanza is called a **couplet**.

- A three-line stanza is called a **tercet**.

- A four-line stanza is called a **quatrain**.

- Stanzas that contain lines of different lengths are called **irregular stanzas**.

I launch this lesson by displaying the Langston Hughes poem "My People":

When I first read a poem, the first thing I notice is how it looks on the page. Some of the things I notice about a poem:

- *Are the lines long or short?*

- *Does the poem have stanzas, or are all the words bunched together?*

- *Are the stanzas even? Do they have the same number of lines?*

- *How much white space surrounds the words?*

Then, when I read the poem, I discover how its structure, especially the stanzas, is entwined with its meaning.

I'm going to share a poem by Langston Hughes called "My People." What do you notice about this poem when you first look at it?

:: My People ::
by Langston Hughes

The night is beautiful.
So, the faces of my people.

The stars are beautiful.
So, the eyes of my people.

Beautiful, also, is the sun.
Beautiful, also, are the souls of my people.

The first thing I notice is that this poem is organized into two-line stanzas, or couplets. As I read a poem, I keep my eyes and ears open so I can notice why I think Langston Hughes used this kind of stanza, the couplet, to write the poem.

As I read the poem aloud, I'm going to read it slowly, pausing between each stanza. I'd like you to visualize in your mind the images the words give you.

After the first reading of the poem, you can ask students to illustrate the poem using three sheets of paper, one for each stanza, and drawing the images they see in their minds. Give students time to draw, and then gather the class together to share and discuss the imagery in each stanza.

Let's start with the title of the poem, "My People." The title gives us a place to start in understanding the meaning of the poem. What does the title tell us about the poem? That's right—we know that the speaker of the poem is referring to his people.

So, why don't you share what you saw in your mind and what you drew for the first stanza. (Some of my students have shared this: "I see the night with the faces of people in the night.")

How about the second stanza? (Sample response: "I see twinkling eyes that are also stars.")

And the third stanza? (Sample response: "I see the sun and pictures of people with their souls rising like the sun.")

So, if we put all the images together, what do you think the poet's message is? (Sample response: "The speaker is comparing the beauty of his people to beautiful images like the night, then the stars, and, finally, the sun.")

Now, let's look at the poem's stanzas. Why do you think Langston Hughes uses couplets, or two-line stanzas, in his poem? How does it support or add meaning to the poem?

Here are some sample responses from my students:

"One line is about the beauty of nature and the next line is about the beauty of his people."

"It shows that, like the night, stars, and the sun—beautiful parts of nature—so his people are beautiful, too. "

"The lines are together because each stanza is a metaphor, and he's comparing nature and his people."

Students often notice that one line in a stanza is about nature and the other line about people, and that putting the two together makes the metaphor even clearer. Also, students have commented about the parallel structure of the lines in each stanza and how Langston Hughes uses the word *so* to connect the first and second image in each stanza.

If you're following the Living With a Poem for One Week model and using this poem, discuss with the class key biographical details of Langston Hughes's life on a Friday. This way, the discussion of the poem and its meaning will have touched upon the key details of the poet's life: the fact that Hughes clearly celebrates African-Americans with the metaphors of the night, stars, and sun. The images in the poem show Hughes's sense of belonging to and pride in his community.

Collaborative Engagement and Independent Application

Use the following activities to extend and assess learning.

Reordering Stanzas

After cutting up the stanzas in "My People" and mixing up the order, ask students to try placing them in order. Then have them explain how the stanzas unfold the poem's meaning.

Choral Reading

"My People" is an excellent poem for choral reading. Use the arrangement of an echo reading (one group reads the first line of the stanza, and the second group reads the second line) to highlight the metaphor and the parallel images in each stanza.

Comparing and Contrasting Texts

Have students compare and contrast the meaning, theme, language, and structure of "My People" with Grace Nichols's poem "They Were My People," cited in the CCSS Appendix B for Grades 4–5 (www.corestandards.org/assets/Appendix_B.pdf). Ask them to research the historical context of both poets' lives and discuss the meaning of the poem through that lens. After students discuss the meaning of the poems with a partner, tell them to look at how the stanzas convey meaning in each poem.

Looking Closely at Stanzas in Exemplar Poems in CCSS Appendix B

Let students choose a poem they like from some of the exemplar poems below in Appendix B for Grades 4–5. After they look closely at the poem's stanzas, have students discuss how the stanzas fit together and progress and help give the poem meaning. Remind students to refer to the types of stanzas they find—couplets, tercets, quatrains, and irregular stanzas—when discussing the meaning of a poem.

"The Echoing Green" by William Blake

"Casey at the Bat" by Ernest Lawrence Thayer

"A Bird Came Down the Walk" by Emily Dickinson

"Fog" by Carl Sandburg

"Dust of Snow" by Robert Frost*

"Little Red Riding Hood and the Wolf" by Roald Dahl*

"They Were My People" by Grace Nichols*

* Text of poem does not appear in CCSS Appendix B.

CHAPTER 12

Text Complexity

My high school English teacher asked us to read and analyze "The Second Coming" by W. B. Yeats. I loved the poem, but when I my paper was returned to me, I was disappointed to find I had received a B– with no explanation. I had no idea why. What was it that I didn't get?

Many of us have read a poem and felt that we just didn't get it and come to the conclusion that there was something wrong with us, or that there was something wrong with poetry. Our teachers often began a poetry study with complex poems and wanted us to interpret them before we knew how to read critically or knew anything about the genre.

One of the key expectations of the CCSS for Reading Literature is that all students should be able to comprehend texts of steadily increasing complexity as they progress through school; the goal is that by the time students graduate, they must be able to read and comprehend independently and proficiently the kinds of complex texts commonly encountered in college and careers.

But what about poetry?

Poetry defies many of the standard qualitative text-complexity measures. A poem can fool us. It can be short, use simple language, and seem completely accessible on first reading, but on rereading, we realize that it has another meaning or that it's written in a traditional form, and without knowledge of that form we wouldn't be able to completely understand its meaning.

For example, the language in Langston Hughes's poem "My People" couldn't be simpler: "The night is beautiful,/So, the faces of my people," but unless readers understand the metaphors in the poem, they won't understand its meaning. In addition, although the poem can be understood without any biographical knowledge of Langston Hughes—the historical time he lived in, and what he witnessed as an African-American during this time—this knowledge is essential in understanding the full meaning of the poem.

Reading poetry is excluded in many literacy programs, except as a quick poetry break or a few weeks during National Poetry Month, so students never progress in reading and explicating increasingly complex poems. In later grades, teachers often introduce poetry by using poems that are far too complex for students, which turns them off poetry.

What Kinds of Poems Should We Be Reading to Our Students?

Of the poetry exemplars in CCSS Appendix B, approximately half are traditional poems written at least 20 years ago, and the other half are contemporary poems.

Since most poetry books and poems have not been leveled, I've adapted the following CCSS qualitative measures to poetry.

- **Levels of Meaning:** Poems with a single level of meaning tend to be easier to read than literary texts with multiple or figurative levels of meaning.

- **Structure:** Poems with low complexity usually have simple structures, such as a regular pattern of rhyme, repetition, rhythm, and stanza or free verse. In addition, a low-complexity poem relates a single event or observation in chronological order and has a single speaker narrating it.

  High-complexity poems tend to have unconventional or highly complex, formal structures (such as a sonnet or villanelle) and employ devices such as flashback, multiple speakers, or multiple events occurring at the same time.

- **Language Conventionality and Clarity:** Poems that are read on the literal level with a clear, familiar, and contemporary speaker using language that is simple and conversational are easier to read than poems that are figurative, obscure, and use traditional, archaic, and sophisticated vocabulary. Many contemporary poems, especially those written for children, are often less complex than poems written prior to the last 20 years, because of the familiar vocabulary.

- **Knowledge Demands: Life Experiences:** Poems that have one simple theme and describe common, everyday experiences from a single perspective are less complex than poems that have multiple themes told from multiple perspectives and out of the realm of students' experiences.

- **Knowledge Demands: Cultural/Literary Knowledge:** Poems that employ commonly known poetic devices such as rhyme, stanza, and rhythm, and free verse poems, and poems about ordinary experiences that students can relate to are easier to read than poems that demand knowledge of more sophisticated poetic devices and that make allusions to other texts.

In addition to these qualitative measures, the quantitative factors that contribute to whether a poem is easy or difficult to read is what the reader brings to the act of reading:

- Motivation (purpose for reading and interest in content)
- Critical analytical ability
- Experience with inferencing
- Experience with and ability to visualize
- Experience with and knowledge of the genre of poetry
- Personal experiences

I believe the most important factor of all is motivation. If a reader feels excited and eager to read a poem, then no matter how complex it is, he or she will make an effort to understand it. Richard Allington said this about nonfiction reading, but I think it applies to poetry as well: "Readers will teach themselves to read . . . [poetry] . . . if they find the subject fascinating."

In read-alouds, we can read more complex poems because our fluent reading and understanding of the poem can convey meaning to students.

"Autumn" by Emily Dickinson is cited as an exemplar text in the CCSS Appendix B in the CCSS for Grade 2 and 3 students.

:: Autumn ::

by Emily Dickinson

The morns are meeker than they were.

The nuts are getting brown;

The berry's cheek is plumper,

The rose is out of town.

The maple wears a gayer scarf,

The field a scarlet gown.

Lest I should be old-fashioned,

I'll put a trinket on.

How would you measure the complexity of this poem on a scale of 1 to 10 (10 being the most complex)? I've completed the chart below to help answer that question.

Low Text Complexity	High Text Complexity
Structure End Rhyme Two Stanzas Regular Meter/Beats	Levels of Meaning Figurative Language: Metaphors

Knowledge Demands
Common Experience
Single Perspective
	Language Conventionality
	  and Clarity
	Archaic vocabulary (*morns,
	  gayer scarf, lest*)

Lyric Poem	

"Autumn" has a fairly simple message, but its old-fashioned and archaic language (*morns, lest*) is tricky for most second- and third-grade students to read independently. Also, the meaning of the poem hinges upon understanding that Dickinson is personifying autumn and the metaphors she uses do this. I'd give it a 6 on the complexity scale.

Although "Autumn" is included in the exemplar texts for second and third grades, the CCSS doesn't expect the study of nonliteral and literal language until Grade 3: RL. 3.4: *Determine the meaning of words and phrases as they are used in a text, distinguishing literal from nonliteral language.* However, language standards L.2.5, L.3.5., L.4.5., and L.5.5. expect students to be able to "Demonstrate understanding of figurative language, word relationships, and nuances in word meanings" in grades 2–5.

In the beginning of the year, many second-grade and most third-grade students find this poem difficult to understand when reading it independently because their comprehension depends upon the following:

- Understanding the archaic vocabulary
- Understanding the metaphor
- Interpreting the metaphor in the last two lines of the poem: "Lest I should be old-fashioned,/I'll put a trinket on."

However, with frequent reading of poems progressing in complexity, experience with reading and analyzing a poem, and explicit mini-lessons on poetic craft such as metaphor, second and third graders are able to understand "Autumn" by the second half of the year.

So begin by introducing and reading poems that have low text complexity—that are immediately accessible to students, written in a contemporary and familiar voice, and relevant to students' lives. As the year progresses, gradually introduce poems of increasing complexity and model comprehension strategies for reading poetry such as those in Chapter 2. Also give demonstration lessons on specific poetic devices. By the end of the year, students should be able to read and understand increasingly complex poems on their own.

CHAPTER 13

The Range of Poems in the CCSS

Just as with music, there is a wide range of types of poetry. The chart below shows the types of literature, including poetry, and informational text that are addressed in the CCSS.

LITERATURE			INFORMATIONAL TEXT
Stories	Drama	Poetry	Literary Nonfiction and Historical, Scientific, and Technical Texts
Includes children's adventure stories, folktales, legends, fables, fantasy, realistic fiction, and myth	Includes staged dialogue and brief familiar scenes	Includes nursery rhymes and the subgenres of the narrative poem, limerick, and free verse poem	Includes biographies and autobiographies; books about history, social studies, science, and the arts; technical texts, including directions, forms, and information displayed in graphs, charts, or maps; and digital sources on a range of topics

In read-alouds, and in the poems we choose for small-group and independent reading, we should consciously offer a variety of types of poems to our students, and teach them the characteristics of the **subgenres** of poetry.

In addition to a range of poetry, we should also read poems to students from other cultures and diverse points of view.

Nursery Rhymes

Nursery rhymes are important for young children because these rhymes help them develop an ear for our language. Both rhyme and rhythm help kids hear the sounds and syllables in the words. Plus, nursery rhymes are part of Western civilization's childhood cultural tradition; yet in many homes, they are not read anymore.

Nursery rhymes originated as poems for young children in Britain and have been passed down from generation to generation because of their mnemonic quality—rhythm and rhyme. Mother Goose rhymes are nursery rhymes, and so are lullabies, which are the oldest children's verse found in every human culture. The musicality and playfulness of nursery rhymes are mesmerizing to children and are part of our cultural history. Some of my favorites include the following:

"Baa Baa Black Sheep"

"Hey Diddle Diddle"

"Jack and Jill"

"Sing a Song of Sixpence"

"Humpty Dumpty"

The Three Subgenres of Poetry: Narrative, Lyric, and Dramatic

Within the main genre of poetry are several subgenres. The CCSS identifies three of them: narrative, lyric, and dramatic.

Narrative Poetry

Narrative comes from the Greek word meaning "story." A **narrative poem** focuses on telling a story. You can often recognize a narrative poem because the point of view is usually second person.

Lyric Poetry

The word *lyric* comes from the Greek meaning "song to the lyre" (a lyre is a musical instrument), which preserves the idea that sound is essential to the lyric poem. The focus of a lyric poem is on the poet's feelings, observations, thoughts, and perceptions. You can recognize a **lyric poem** because most are written from the perspective of the speaker, in the first person. Although a lyric poem can tell a story or relate an event, it differs from a narrative poem in that its focus is on the poet observing the story; in a narrative poem, the focus is on the story itself.

Dramatic Poetry

A **dramatic poem** is a drama that's written in verse or in poetic form, such as the plays of Shakespeare.

Limerick

A **limerick** is a humorous nonsense poem that was made famous by Edward Lear in his brilliant *Book of Nonsense* (1845). It's a fun form for students to read and to try writing. Here is an explanation of its complicated structure:

- The standard limerick is a stanza of five lines.
- The last words of the first, second, and fifth lines rhyme with one another.
- The last words in the third and fourth lines rhyme with each other.

To make it more complicated—the first, second, and fifth lines have this rhythm pattern: da da DUM da da DUM da da DUM (approximately three da da DUMS, or feet, of three syllables each). The defining "foot" of a limerick's meter is called **anapest** (da-da-DUM). The shorter third and fourth lines have this rhythm pattern: da DUM da da DUM.

Here is an example of one of my limerick attempts with a few variations on the meter:

> There once was a fellow named Dude
> who was always in a bad mood.
> He kicked a tree
> and was stung by a bee
> and that made him even more rude.

Free Verse

Free verse is poetry that is written without the use of strict meter or rhyme that uses the natural rhythms of speech.

Correlation of Poems in the Text to CCSS

Although the poems included in this book are used in lessons to demonstrate specific standards, they can also be used with myriad other English Language Standards. I've included a list of all the relevant standards that are applicable to each poem in the chart below.

Title/Poet	Standards Application	Chapter/Page
"Ducks on a Winter's Night" by Georgia Heard	RL.2.4, 3.4, K.5, 4.5; FS 3.4, 4.4, 5.4; SL.K.5, 1.5, 2.5, 3.5; L.K.5, 1.5, 2.5, 3.5, 4.5, 5.5	Chapter 2, page 23
"Enchantment" by Joanne Ryder	RL.1.4, 2.4, 3.4, 5.4; FS. 3.4, 3.5, 4.5, 5.5; SL.2.5, 3.5,; L.2.5, 4.5, 5.5	Chapter 2, page 29
"We Are Trees" by Francisco X. Alarcón	RL.4.2, 5.2, 3.4, 5.4, K.5, 3.5, 4.5, 5.5; FS.3.4, 4.4, 5.4; SL.2.5, 3.5; L.1.5, 2.5, 3.5, 4.5, 5.5	Chapter 2, page 36
"Sound of Water" by Mary O'Neill	RL.1.4, 2.4, K.5, 4.5, 5.5; FS.3.4, 4.4, 5.4; SL.2.5, 3.5; L.K.5, 1.5, 2.5, 3.5, 4.5, 5.5	Chapter 3, page 39
"My Horse and I" by Georgia Heard	RL.1.4, 2.4, K.5, 4.5, 5.5; FS.3.4, 4.4, 5.4; SL.2.5, 3.5; L.K.5, 1.5, 2.5, 3.5, 4.5, 5.5	Chapter 3, page 40
"Ears Hear" by Lucia M. Hymes and James L. Hymes, Jr.	RL.1.4, 2.4, K.5, 3.5, 4.5, 5.5; FS.3.4, 4.4, 5.4; SL.2.5, 3.5; L.1.5, 2.5, 3.5; L.1.5, 2.5, 3.5	Chapter 4, page 51
"Ice Cream Cone" by Heidi E. Y. Stemple	RL.1.4, 2.4, K.5, 3.5, 5.5; FS.K.4, 1.4, 2.4, 3.4, 4.4, 5.4; SL.2.5, 3.5; L.K.5, 1.5, 2.5, 3.5	Chapter 4, page 52
"A Circle of Sun" by Rebecca Kai Dotlich	RL.4.2, 5.2, 1.4, 2.4, 3.4, 5.4, K.5, 4.5; FS.3.4, 4.4, 5.4; SL.2.5, 3.5; L.1.5, 2.5, 3.5, 4.5, 5.5	Chapter 4, page 55
"When I Was Lost" by Dorothy Aldis	RL.1.4, 2.4, 3.4, 5.4, 2.5, 3.5, 4.5, 5.5; FS.3.4, 4.4, 5.4; SL.2.5, 3.5; L.1.5, 2.5, 3.5, 4.5, 5.5;	Chapter 4, page 56

"Eagle Flight" by Georgia Heard	RL.2.4, 3.4, 4.5, 5.4; FS.3.4, 4.4, 5.4; SL.2.5, 3.5; L.2.5, 3.5, 4.5, 5.5	Chapter 5, page 60
"Song of the Dolphin" by Georgia Heard	RL.2.4, 3.5, 4.5, 5.5; FS.K.4, 1.4, 2.4, 3.4, 4.4, 5.4; SL.2.5, 3.5	Chapter 5, page 61
"Ode to the Washing Machine" by Rebecca Kai Dotlich	RL.2.4, 3.4, 5.4, 3.5, 4.5, 5.5; FS.3.4, 4.4, 5.4; SL.2.5, 3.5; L.2.5, 3.5, 4.5, 5.5	Chapter 5, page 64
"Summer Snakes" by Georgia Heard	RL.2.4, K.5; FS.K.4, 1.4, 2.4, 3.4, 4.4, 5.4; SL.2.5, 3.5	Chapter 5, page 64
"Favorite Bear" by Georgia Heard	RL.2.4, 3.5, 4.5, 5.5; FS.3.4, 4.4, 5.4; SL.2.5, 3.5; L.K.5, 1.5, 2.5	Chapter 5, page 66
"Bat Patrol" by Georgia Heard	RL.2.4, 3.4, 5.4, 3.5, 4.5, 5.5; FS.3.4, 4.4, 5.4; SL.2.5, 3.5; L.2.5, 3.5, 4.5, 5.5	Chapter 5, page 68
"Dragonfly" by Rebecca Kai Dotlich	RL.1.4, 2.4, 3.4, 5.4; FS.3.4, 4.4, 5.4; SL.2.5, 3.5; L.2.5, 3.5, 4.5, 5.5	Chapter 6, page 73
"A Modern Dragon" by Rowena Bastin Bennett	RL.1.4, 2.4, 3.4, 5.4, 4.5; FS.3.4, 4.4, 5.4; SL.2.5, 3.5; L.2.5, 3.5, 4.5, 5.5	Chapter 7, page 77
"Ditchdiggers" by Lydia Pender	RL.1.4, 2.4, 3.4, 5.4, 4.5; FS.3.4, 4.4, 5.4; SL.2.5, 3.5; L.2.5, 3.5, 4.5, 5.5	Chapter 7, page 78
"Oak Tree" by Georgia Heard	RL.3.4, 5.4, K.5, 4.5; FS.K.4, 1.4, 2.4, 3.4, 4.4, 5.4; SL.2.5, 3.5; L.K.5, 1.5, 2.5, 3.5	Chapter 8, page 86
"Saturday" by Kay Winters	RL.1.4, 2.4, 3.4, K.5, 3.5; FS.K.4, 1.4, 2.4, 3.4; SL.2.5, 3.5; L.K.5, 1.5, 2.5, 3.5	Chapter 8, page 88
"Sand House" by J. Patrick Lewis	RL.2.4, 3.4, K.5, 3.5, 4.5; FS.K.4, 1.4, 2.4, 3.4, 4.4, 5.4; SL.2.5, 3.5 ; L.2.5, 3.5, 4.5, 5.5	Chapter 9, page 92
"My People" by Langston Hughes	RL.2.4, 3.4, 5.4, 3.5, 5.5; FS.3.4, 4.4, 5.4; SL.2.5, 3.5; L.2.5, 3.5 4.5, 5.5	Chapter 11, page 104
"Autumn" by Emily Dickinson	RL.2.4, 3.4, 5.4, 3.5, 4.5, 5.5; FS.2.4, 3.4, 4.4, 5.4; SL.3.5, 4.5, 5.5; L2.5, 3.5, 4.5, 5.5	Chapter 12, page 109

Name: _____ Date: _____

5W and H Thinking Map

Title: _____ Author: _____

WHO?	WHAT?
• speaker or person named in poem • point of view • tone • speaker's voice	• What's happening in the poem? • Does the poem express a feeling, action, observation, thought, etc.?
WHERE?	WHEN?
• Where does the poem or its events take place?	• When does the poem or its events take place?
WHY?	HOW?
• Why do you think the poet wrote this poem? • What's the purpose of the poem?	• How is the poem made? • What craft tools does the poet use?
QUESTIONS	PERSONAL CONNECTIONS

Guided Craft Question Sheet

Title: _____ Author: _____

Sound: Which sound patterns (*repetition, alliteration, rhyme, rhythm*) does the poem contain? Highlight them. Can you identify them by name?	**Stanza:** Does the poem have any stanzas? How does each stanza build the poem? How does the last stanza bring the ideas of the poem together?
Imagery: What pictures do you see in your mind as you read the poem? What can you see, hear, taste, touch, and smell? What are some of the words, phrases, and lines that help the poem come alive?	**Figurative Language:** Can you identify any figurative language? How does the figurative language add to the poem? Is there a deeper meaning than what's on the surface of the poem?
Words: Which words feel important or surprising? Highlight them. Underline the words you need to look up.	**Form:** What are the structural elements of the poem? How do they contribute to the poem?

Name: _____   Date: _____

Poetry Reading Pre-Assessment Sheet

Title: _____ Author: _____

Read the poem carefully several times. Then answer the questions as thoughtfully as you can.

What makes this a poem?

_____

_____

_____

_____

What is this poem about? What is the poet's message (big idea)?

_____

_____

_____

_____

What tools do you notice the poet is using to help show his or her message?

_____

_____

_____

_____

Name: _____   Date: _____

Five Senses Word Sheet

Title: _____ Author: _____

Look for sense words, phrases, or lines in the poem. Write them on a sticky note.
Place the sticky note in the correct box.

See	Hear
Touch	**Taste**
Smell	

Name: _____ Date: _____

Musical Tools Reading Sheet

Title: _____ Poet: _____

Regular Beats/Rhythm	Alliteration
Rhymes	**Repeated Lines**

Name: _____ Date: _____

Figurative Language Reading Sheet

Title: _____ Poet: _____

Nonliteral Words (Figurative Language)	Literal Words (Facts)

Name: _____ Date: _____

Visualization Sheet

Strong readers make pictures in their minds to understand the meaning of a poem.
Draw your mind pictures in the box.

I think that the poet's message is:

_____

_____

_____ .

alliteration: the repetition of consonant or vowel sounds at the beginning of words close together; *Example: Pease Porridge* (see also *assonance* and *consonance*)

assonance: the repetition of internal vowel sounds in words close together; *Example: I made a cake today.*

blank verse: unrhymed verse

concrete poem: a poem shaped like the specific object it describes

consonance: the repetition of internal or ending consonant sounds in words close together; *Example: litter/batter, dress/boss*

couplet: a stanza of two lines

dramatic monologue: a poem written in the form of a speech of an individual character

dramatic poem: a drama written in verse or poetry form

end rhyme: rhyme occurring at the end of two or more lines

end-stopped: when the poet completes a thought, action, or image at the end of a line

enjambment: the continuation of a sentence or a clause over a line break so that closely related words fall in different lines

exact rhyme: a repetition of similar sounds in which all the letters, except the first, are identical; *Example: hot, pot.*

explication: from the Latin *explicaire*: to unfold, to fold out, or to make clear the meaning of; usually involves a line-by-line reading and commentary on what is going on in a poem, finding evidence to support our ideas, and referring to that evidence as we speak and write about the poem

figurative language: figures of speech; literary devices, such as simile and metaphor

foot: a group of stressed and unstressed syllables combining to form a unit of verse; a rhythm unit in a line of poetry

formal poetry: poetry that follows "rules" regarding stanza length and number of rhyme patterns and that uses fixed forms; *Example: A sonnet is either 14 or 16 lines and is written in iambic pentameter.*

free verse: poetry that makes use of natural cadences rather than a fixed metrical pattern. The rhythmical lines vary in length and are usually unrhymed; though it may appear unrestrained, there is a firm pattern to the words.

iamb or iambic: the most common meter in the English language, consisting of an unstressed syllable and a stressed syllable written like this *u/*

iambic pentameter: five iambs on one line

imagery: the use of sensory details or images that appeal to one or more of the five senses; a word or phrase that creates pictures in the reader's mind and helps the reader understand the poem

internal rhyme: rhyme that occurs within a line (or lines) instead of at the end

irregular stanzas: stanzas that contain lines of different lengths

limerick: a five-line form of humorous verse with an a-a-b-b-a rhyme scheme

line or verse: a single row of words appearing together on a line, considered as a unit

line break: the end of a line of poetry

lyric poem: a poem that focuses on the poet's feelings, observations, thoughts, and perceptions, and utilizes the sound of words

metaphor: a statement that compares one thing, or image, to another without using *like* or *as*

meter: the regular rhythmic pattern in a poem; the arrangement of beats or accents in a line of poetry designated by a pattern of stressed and unstressed syllables that helps establish the rhythm of a poem; common meters in poetry:

- **trochee:** DA/dum /u
- **spondee:** DA/DA //
- **anapest:** da da/DUM uu/
- **dactyl:** DA/dum/dum /uu

narrative poem: a poem that focuses on telling a story

onomatopoeia: the use of words that imitate sounds and suggest their meaning; *Examples: Bam! Ow! Sizzle! Zip!*

personification: the attribution of a human quality to an inanimate object, plant, or animal

prose: ordinary speech or writing, as distinguished from verse. Prose closely corresponds to patterns of everyday speech; when written, it follows conventions of print, such as sentences, paragraphs, indenting, and punctuation.

prosody: the study of meter in poetry

quatrain: a four-line stanza

refrain: a line or lines that are repeated in a poem

repetition or repeated lines: the reoccurrence of sounds, words, phrases, or lines in a poem, adding rhythm and interest to a poem

rhyme: the repetition of the same or similar vowel and consonant sounds in two or more words, usually at the end of words

rhyme scheme: a consistent pattern of rhyme found in a stanza or poem

rhythm: in poetry, rhythm is made up of sound and silences that together form a pattern of sounds. The beat of the poem is the rhythm in which the syllables fall.

run-on line: a line in which the thought, action, or image continues onto the next line

scan: reading a poem to find its meter

simile: the comparison between one thing and another using the word *like* or *as*

slant rhyme: rhymes that are close but not exact; *Example: twist and kiss*

sonnet: a formal poem with either 14 or 16 lines, depending on what kind of sonnet it is, and written in iambic pentameter

stanza: the grouping together of lines arranged according to a fixed plan, such as line length or rhyme scheme; stanzas are set apart by blank space.

subgenre: a type of poetry that includes narrative, lyric, and dramatic

tercet: a stanza with three lines

theme: the general topic or subject of a poem or poet's message

verse: a single line of poetry, or another word for poetry, especially poetry that is metrical and rhymed

villanelle: a poem with 19 lines consisting of five tercets and a final quatrain on two rhymes.

Poems and Books Cited in Text

Alarcón, Francisco X. (2005). "We Are Trees" in *Laughing tomatoes: and other spring poems*. San Francisco: Children's Book Press.

Alexander, Elizabeth. (2005 October/November). "An Interview with Rita Dove." Retrieved August 13, 2011, from www.awpwriter.org/library/writers_chronicle_view/1786/an_interview_with_rita_dove.

Allen, Judy. (2004). *Are You a Dragonfly?* Boston: Houghton Mifflin.

Angelou, Maya. (1978). "Still I Rise" in *And still I rise*. New York: Random House.

Bach, Gerhard, & Hall, Blaine H. (Eds.). (1997). *Conversations with Grace Paley*. Jackson, MS: University Press of Mississippi.

Blake, William. (1971). "The Echoing Green" in *Songs of innocence*. New York: Dover.

Blake, William. (1994). "The Tyger" in *Blake: Poems* (Everyman's Library Pocket Poets). New York: Everyman's Library.

Calkins, L., Ehrenworth, M., & Lehman, C. (2012). *Pathways to the Common Core: Accelerating achievement*. Portsmouth, NH: Heinemann.

Collins, Billy. (1988). "Introduction to Poetry" in *The Apple that astonished Paris*. Fayetteville, AR: University of Arkansas Press.

Collins, Billy. (2002). "Litany" in *Nine Horses*. New York: Random House.

Collopy, Trisha. (2011, November). "In an age of instant communication, poetry invites people to slow down." *The Council Chronicle*, pp. 20–21.

Creech, Sharon. (2001). *Love that dog*. New York: HarperCollins.

Creech, Sharon. (2010). *Hate that cat*. New York: HarperCollins.

Dahl, Roald. (2002). "Little Red Riding Hood and the Wolf" in *Revolting rhymes*. New York: Knopf.

Dakos, Kalli. (1995). *If you're not here, please raise your hand: Poems about school*. New York: Simon & Schuster Books for Young Readers.

Davies, Nicola (2001). *Bat loves the night*. Somerville, MA: Candlewick Press.

Davies, Nicola. (2012). *Outside your window: A first book of nature*. Somerville, MA: Candlewick.

Dickinson, Emily. (1960). "Autumn," "A Bird Came Down the Walk" in Thomas H. Johnson (Ed.), *The complete poems of Emily Dickinson*. New York: Little Brown.

Dotlich, Rebecca Kai. (2010). "Ode to the Washing Machine" in *In the spin of things: Poetry of motion*. Honesdale, PA: Wordsong.

Dotlich, Rebecca Kai. (2000). *Sweet dreams of the wild: Poems for bedtime*. Honesdale, PA: Boyds Mills.

Dotlich, Rebecca Kai. (1998). "Dragonfly," and "A Circle of Sun" in *Lemonade sun: And other summer poems*. Honesdale, PA: Wordsong.

Dotlich, Rebecca Kai. (2004). *Over in the pink house: New jump rope rhymes*. Honesdale, PA: Boyds Mills.

Ferris, Helen (Ed.). (1957). "The New Colossus" by Emma Lazarus and "Casey at the Bat" in Helen Ferris (Ed.), *Favorite poems old and new*. New York: Doubleday.

Field, Rachel. (1934). "Something Told the Wild Geese" in *Branches green*. New York: Macmillan.

Fletcher, Ralph. (2010). *Pyrotechnics on the page: Playful craft that sparks writing*. Portsmouth, NH: Heinemann.

Florian, Douglas. (2003). *Autumnblings*. New York: Greenwillow.

Florian, Douglas. (2006). *Handsprings*. New York: Greenwillow.

Florian, Douglas. (2002). *Summersaults*. New York: Greenwillow.

Florian, Douglas. (1999). *Winter eyes*. New York: Greenwillow.

Franco, Betsy. (2006). *Math poetry: Linking language and math in a fresh way*. Tucson: Good Year Books.

Freese, Susan. (2008). *Carrots to cupcakes: Reading, writing, and reciting poems about food*. Minneapolis: Super Sandcastle.

Frost, Robert. (1969). "After Apple Picking," "Dust of Snow" in *The poetry of Robert Frost: The collected poems, complete and unabridged*. New York: Henry Holt.

Frost, Robert. (1979). "Stopping by Woods on a Snowy Evening" in Edward Connery Lathem (Ed.), *The poetry of Robert Frost: The collected poems*. New York: Henry Holt.

Frost, Robert. (2011). "Birches" in *Mountain interval*. Charleston, SC: CreateSpace.

Frye, N. (1963). *The well-tempered critic*. Bloomington, IN: Indiana University Press.

Harper, Michael. (2009, April 27). Retrieved September 16, 2011, from www.mamkschools.org/education/components.

Heard, Georgia. (1997). "Ducks on a Winter's Night," "Bat Patrol," "Favorite Bear," "Song of the Dolphin, "Eagle Flight" in *Creatures of earth, sea, and sky: Animal poems*. Honesdale: PA: Wordsong.

Heard, G., & Laminack, L. (2007). *Climb inside a poem: Reading and writing poetry across the school day*. Portsmouth, NH: FirstHand.

Heard, Georgia. (1998). *Awakening the heart: Exploring poetry in elementary and middle school*. Portsmouth, NH: Heinemann.

Heard, Georgia. (2009). "Oak Tree" in *Falling down the page: A book of list poems*. New York: Roaring Brook Press.

Heard, Georgia & McDonough, Jennifer. (2009). *A place for wonder: Reading and writing nonfiction in the primary grades*. Portland, ME: Stenhouse.

Heard, Georgia. (2002). *The revision toolbox: Teaching techniques that work*. Portsmouth, NH: Heinemann.

Helakoski, Leslie. (2006). *Big chickens*. New York: Dutton.

Hirsch, Edward. (1999). *How to read a poem and fall in love with poetry*. Orlando: Harcourt.

Hoberman, Mary Ann. (2006). *You read to me, I'll read to you*. New York: Little, Brown.

Hoberman, M., & Winston, L. (Eds.). (2009). *The tree that time built: A celebration of nature, science, and imagination*. Naperville, IL: Sourcebooks.

Hoberman, Mary Ann. (2012). *Forget-Me-Nots: Poems to learn by heart*. New York: Little, Brown.

Hopkins, Lee Bennett. (Ed.). (2011). *I am the book*. New York: Holiday House.

Hopkins, Lee Bennett. (Ed.). (2001). *Marvelous math: A Book of poems*. New York: Simon & Schuster.

Hopkins, Lee Bennett. (2000). *School supplies*. New York: Aladdin.

Hopkins, Lee Bennett. (Ed.). (2002). *Spectacular science: A book of poems*. New York: Simon & Schuster.

Hopkins, Lee Bennett. (Ed.). (1995). *Weather: Poems for all seasons*. New York: HarperCollins.

Hopkins, Lee Bennett. (Ed.). (2004). *Wonderful words: Poems about reading, writing, speaking, and listening*. New York: Simon & Schuster.

Hughes, Langston. (1994.) "Harlem," "Poem" in Arnold Rampersad (Ed.), *The collected poems of Langston Hughes*. New York: Knopf.

Hughes, Langston. (2009). *My people*. New York: Atheneum.

Jarrell, Randall. (1964). "A Bat Is Born" in *The bat poet*. New York: HarperCollins.

Jensen, Dana. (2012). *A meal of the stars: Poems up and down*. Boston: Houghton Mifflin.

Johnson, Georgia Douglas. (2001). "Your World" in Belinda Rochelle (Ed.), *Words with wings: A treasury of African-American poetry and art*. New York: HarperCollins.

Laminack, Lester L. (2004). *Saturdays and teacakes*. Atlanta: Peachtree.

Langstaff, John. (1973). *Over in the meadow*. Boston: Houghton Mifflin.

Lear, Edward. (1845). *Book of nonsense*. London: Thomas McLean.

Levertov, Denise. (1968.) "Origins of a poem" in *The poet in the world. The Michigan Quarterly Review 7*(4). Ann Arbor, MI: University of Michigan Press.

Lewis, Patrick J. (2002). *Aritheme-Tickle: An even number of odd riddle-rhymes*. Orlando: Harcourt.

Lionni, Leo. (1967). *Frederick*. New York: Alfred A. Knopf.

Lopez, Alonzo. (1997). "Celebration" in Lee Bennett Hopkins (Ed.), *Song and dance*. New York: Simon & Schuster.

Mannis, Celeste Davidson. (2002). *One leaf rides the wind: A Japanese counting book*. New York: Viking.

Millay, Edna St. Vincent. (2001). "Afternoon on a Hill" in Nancy Milford (Ed.), *The selected poetry of Edna St. Vincent Millay*. New York: Modern Library.

Moore, Lilian. (1982). "Wind Song" in *Something new begins*. New York: Atheneum.

Mora, Pat. (1996). "Words Free As Confetti" in *Confetti: Poems for children*. New York: Lee & Low Books.

Moss, Lloyd. (1995). *Zin! Zin! Zin! A violin*. New York: Simon & Schuster.

Newkirk, T. (2011). *The art of slow reading: Six time-honored practices for engagement*. Portsmouth, NH: Heinemann.

Nichols, Grace. (1990. "They Were My People" in *Come on into my tropical garden*. New York: HarperCollins.

Nye, Naomi Shihab. (Ed.). (1992). *This same sky: A collection of poems from around the world*. New York: Four Winds Press.

O'Neill, Mary. (1984). "Sound of Water" in Joanna Cole (Ed.), *A new treasury of children's poetry: Old favorites and new discoveries*. New York: Doubleday.

Prelutsky, Jack. (Ed.). (2007). *Good sports: Rhymes about running, jumping, throwing, and more*. New York: Knopf.

Prelutsky, Jack. (Ed.). (1999). "Ears Hear" by Lucia M. Hymes and James L. Hymes, Jr., "September" by John Updike, "Scarecrow Complains" by Lilian Moore, "Tiger" by Valerie Worth, "Until I Saw the Sea" by Lilian Moore, "When I Was Lost" by Dorothy Aldis (from *All Together*, 1925), "Moving" by Eileen Spinelli, "Mad Song" by Myra Cohn Livingston, "The Bad Mood Bug" by Brod Bagert, "If a Bad Dream Comes" by Siv Cedering Fox, "And My Heart Soars" by Chief Dan George, "Singing-Time" by Rose Fyleman, "By Myself" by Eloise Greenfield, "Covers" by Nikki Giovanni, "A Modern Dragon" by Rowena Bastin Bennett, "Ditchdiggers" by Lydia Pender in *The 20th Century Children's Treasury of Poetry*. New York: Alfred A. Knopf.

Prelutsky, Jack. (2012, April 12). "'A poem is a living organism, and no two are alike.'" Interview with Maryann Yin in *Galleycat*. Retrieved September 14, 2012, from http://www.mediabistro.com/galleycat/jack-prelutsky-on-how-the-internet-inspired-his-poetry_b50059.

Rosenblatt, L. M. (1978). *The reader, the text, the poem: The transactional theory of the literary work*. Carbondale, IL: Southern Illinois University Press.

Ross, Mandy. (2005). *Wake up, sleepy head! Early morning poems (poems for the young)*. Swindon, Wiltshire, U.K.: Childs Play Intl.

Ryder, Joanne. (1990). "Enchantment" in Paul B. Janeczko (Ed.), *The place my words are looking for: What poets say about and through their work*. New York: Bradbury Press.

Rylant, Cynthia. (1991). *Night in the country*. New York: Atheneum.

Salas, Laura Purdie. (2012). *Bookspeak! Poems about books*. New York: Clarion.

Sandburg, Carl. (1916). "Fog" in *Chicago poems*. New York: Henry Holt.

Schenk de Regniers, Beatrice; Moore, Eva; White, Mary Michaels; & Carr, Jan. (Eds.). (1988). "Knoxville, Tennessee" by Nikki Giovanni, "Weather" by Eve Merriam, "Who Has Seen the Wind?" by Christina Rossetti. New York: Scholastic.

Shakespeare, William. (2002). "Sonnet 18" in Colin Burrow (Ed.), *The Oxford Shakespeare complete sonnets and poems*. New York: Oxford University Press.

Shaw, Nancy. (2005). *Raccoon tune*. New York: Holt & Co.

Showers, Paul. (1993). *The listening walk*. New York: HarperCollins.

Sidman, Joyce. (2009). *Red sings from treetops: A year in colors*. Boston: Houghton Mifflin.

Soto, Gary. (1995). "Eating While Reading" in *Canto familiar*. Boston: Houghton Mifflin Harcourt Publishing Company.

Thomas, Lewis. (1990). *Et cetera, et cetera: Notes on a word-watcher*. Boston: Little, Brown and Company.

Winters, Kay. (2001). "Saturday" in *Did you see what I saw? Poems about school*. New York: Puffin Books.

Worth, Valerie. (1994). "Sweets" in *All the small poems and fourteen more*. New York: Farrar, Straus & Giroux.

Worth, Valerie. (1996). "Coins" and "Aquarium" in *All the small poems and fourteen more*. New York: Farrar, Straus and Giroux.

Wright, Richard. (1994). "Laughing Boy" in Barbara Rogasky (Ed.), *Winter poems*. New York: Scholastic.

Yolen, Jane. (1987). *Owl moon*. New York: Philomel.

Yolen, Jane. (Ed.). (2007). "Ice Cream Cone" by Heidi E. Y. Stemple, "Cat Kisses" by Bobbi Katz, "Manhattan Lullaby" by Norma Farber, "The NO-NO Bird" by Andrew Fusek Peters, "Mud" by Flanders and Swann, "Sand House" by J. Patrick Lewis in *Here's a little poem: A very first poetry book*. Somerville, MA: Candlewick.

Yolen, Jane. (2010). *Switching on the moon: A very first book of bedtime poems*. Somerville, MA: Candlewick Press.

Recommended Poetry Books and Anthologies

Angelou, Maya. (2007). *Poetry for young people: Maya Angelou.* Dr. Edwin Graves Wilson (Ed.). New York: Sterling.

Corcoran, Jill. (Ed.). (2012). *Dare to dream . . . change the world.* La Jolla, CA: Kane/Miller.

Dickinson, Emily. (1994). *Poetry for young people: Emily Dickinson.* Frances Schoonmaker Bolin (Ed.). New York: Sterling.

Dotlich, Rebecca Kai. (2001). *When riddles come rumbling: Poems to ponder.* Honesdale, PA: Wordsong.

Fletcher, Ralph. (2005). *A writing kind of day: Poems for young poets.* Honesdale, PA: Boyds Mills Press.

Florian, Douglas. (2001). *Lizards, frogs, and polliwogs.* New York: Harcourt.

Florian, Douglas. (2012). *unBEElievables: Honeybee poems and paintings.* New York: Simon & Schuster.

Frost, Helen. (2012). *Step gently out.* Somerville, MA: Candlewick Press.

Frost, Robert. (2008). *Poetry for young people: Robert Frost.* Gary D. Schmidt (Ed.). New York: Sterling.

George, Kristine O'Connell. (2011). *Emma Dilemma: Big sister poems.* New York: Clarion.

Giovanni, Nikki. (2008) *Hip hop speaks to children: A celebration of poetry with a beat.* Naperville, IL: Sourcebooks.

Harrison, David L. (2000). *Farmer's garden: Rhymes for two voices.* Honesdale, PA: Wordsong.

Holbrook, Sara. (2011). *Weird? (Me, too!) Let's be friends.* Honesdale, PA: Wordsong.

Hoyte, Carol-Ann, & Roemer, Heidi Bee. (Eds.). (2012). *And the crowd goes wild! A global gathering of sports poems.* Victoria BC, Canada: FriesenPress.

Hubbell, Patricia. (2001). *City kids.* New York: Cavendish.

Janeczko, Paul. (1999). *Very best (almost) friends: Poems of friendship.* Somerville, MA: Candlewick Press.

Janeczko, Paul. (2009). *A kick in the head: An everyday guide to poetic forms.* Somerville, MA: Candlewick Press.

Janeczko, Paul. (2009). *A foot in the mouth: Poems to speak, sing and shout.* Somerville, MA: Candlewick Press.

Nye, Naomi Shihab. (1998). *The tree is older than you are: A bilingual gathering of poems & stories from Mexico with paintings by Mexican artists.* New York: Aladdin.

Nye, Naomi Shihab. (2005). *19 varieties of gazelle: Poems of the Middle East.* New York: Greenwillow.

Sandburg, Carl. (2008). *Poetry for young people: Carl Sandburg.* Frances Schoonmaker Bolin (Ed.). New York: Sterling.

Schertle, Alice. (1997). *A lucky thing.* Orlando, FL: Harcourt Brace.

Singer, Marilyn. (2010). *Mirror mirror: A book of reversible verse.* New York: Dutton.

Singer, Marilyn. (2012). *A stick is an excellent thing: Poems celebrating outdoor play.* New York: Clarion.

Vardell, Sylvia, & Wong, Janet. (2012). *The Poetry Friday anthology: Poems for the school year with connections to the Common Core.* Princeton, NJ: Pomelo Books.

Wong, Janet. (2012). *Declaration of interdependence: Poems for an election year.* Princeton, NJ: Poetry-Suitcase.com.

Recommended Poetry Web Sites

Academy of American Poets: www.poets.org

Favorite Poem Project: www.favoritepoem.org

KidLitosphere Central: www.kidlitosphere.org

Poetry Daily: www.poems.com

Poetry Everywhere: www.pbs.org/wgbh/poetryeverywhere/

Poetry for Children blog: poetryforchildren.blogspot.com

Poetry Foundation: www.poetryfoundation.org

Poetry 180: www.loc.gov/poetry/180/

Poetry Out Loud: www.poetryoutloud.org/

Rhyming Dictionary: www.rhymezone.com